EDWARD CARPENTER

EDWARD CARPENTER

A Victorian Rebel Fighting for Gay Rights

BRIAN ANDERSON

Matador
9 Priory Business Park,
Wistow Road, Kibworth Beauchamp,
Leicestershire. LE8 0RX
Tel: 0116 279 2299
Email: books@troubador.co.uk
Web: www.troubador.co.uk/matador
Twitter: @matadorbooks

ISBN 978 1800463 912

British Library Cataloguing in Publication Data.
A catalogue record for this book is available from the British Library.

Printed and bound by CPI Group (UK) Ltd, Croydon, CR0 4YY
Typeset in 11pt Aldine401 BT by Troubador Publishing Ltd, Leicester, UK

Matador is an imprint of Troubador Publishing Ltd

For Martin and Mafruha

Contents

He will never be forgotten as a pioneer in living almost openly a homosexual life, which needed a rare combination of skill and courage; and retaining throughout the honour and respect of the world. He succeeded where Oscar Wilde miserably failed.

Havelock Ellis

Introduction

The term 'gay liberation' is now applied almost exclusively to the period from the late 1960s, through to the mid-1980s, during which homosexuals engaged in direct action against social and legal oppression. Sparked by the Stonewall riots in Greenwich Village, Manhattan, in June 1969, it became part of an American counter-culture. In England, a Gay Liberation Front (GLF) was founded in October 1970, again with a radical manifesto going beyond the reform of laws against homosexuality, to demands for fundamental changes in the status of homosexuals in society.

What is not widely known, particularly in the LGBTQ community, is that this fight for gay liberation in England began much earlier, in the last decade of the Victorian era. On the west side of Brunswick Square, on the cusp of Brighton and Hove in East Sussex, is number 45, a large elegant Regency house, where a plaque on the stonework names it as the birthplace of Edward Carpenter, described simply as a writer. It is ironic, that in Brighton, a very gay city, few seem aware of the rebellious life of this upper-middle-class Victorian gentleman, who, almost alone, opened the fight for the legal recognition of same-sex love that would not be achieved in England until 1967, and then only partially.

Leading a sheltered life as a Cambridge don and Anglican curate, 'Chips' Carpenter seemed the least likely of individuals prepared to court notoriety as a defender of homosexuality. But, in Carpenter, we meet a rare kind of Victorian: an individual who accepted his sexual nature and, if slowly and painfully, came to regard himself as a 'normal' man. In a society with deeply ambivalent attitudes towards sexuality, particularly to all forms of male lust, he made his own sexual temperament a little-disguised fact. He was alone of his generation in publicly affirming his sexuality, and in refusing to lead a double life of conformity and surreptitious deviancy. He chose the hard way: to put the case for himself and his kind. Many of his prominent contemporaries who were homosexual, men such as John Addington Symonds, Edmund Gosse, A. E. Housman and Walter Pater, struggled with their sexuality and lived secretive lives. Others departed England's shores for the freer sexual climate of southern Europe.

At the very time Oscar Wilde was languishing in Reading Jail, and the homosexual was being publicly excoriated, Carpenter set out to construct an essentially non-sexualised homosexual identity; one that detached the 'innate homosexual bias' from 'carnal curiosity'. He did not ask simply for tolerance for such a love, a plea that would become the central concern of sexual liberationists in the following century. Instead, he sought recognition of the *homosexual* impulse, not as a recurrent vice, but as a natural variant of human sexuality.

The mid-century reform of the English public schools ushered in a cult of ostentatious masculinity, which made all forms of homosociality suspect. In 1885, Parliament had extended the scope of the law governing homosexual acts, making even an embrace or innocent kiss between two men punishable by up to two years' imprisonment for 'gross indecency'. It reflected a collective fear of the destructive power of uncontrolled sexual passion. Sex was banished from public discourse, but surfaced in the form of prudery, pornography, theatre censorship, the expurgation of art and the bowdlerising and prosecution of books for obscenity.

In the face of such strong cultural taboos, Carpenter sought to raise public awareness of homosexuality, and to argue for the value of the homosexual to society. It was a time of growing recognition of a sphere of privacy for the satisfaction of individual wants; where personal choice, not religious, moral or social strictures, was sovereign. As such, Carpenter argued, homosexual desire could not be denied legitimacy as an element of personal self-fulfilment and happiness.

What he embarked upon was dangerous and he was always vulnerable. His co-habitation with another man was scandalising and his writing alerted him to the authorities as a person to be watched. His defence against prosecution was a disarming kind of obfuscation. His innocuous, often anodyne, prose was a beguiling cover for the exposition of matters on which it was unwise to speak, let alone write. He was the subtle persuader, the rhetorical questioner gently mocking the bigoted. His method was collusion with his readers, with their empathy and with their reasonableness. There was a calm, matter-of-fact, unashamed celebration of the homosexual's right to exist.

Remarkably, the extent of his sexual radicalism was not limited to challenging the taboo against homosexuality. Believing that sexual fulfilment was a primary human need, he was one of the first men to acknowledge women's erotic natures, and to argue for the breaking of the link between sex and procreation. His 1896 book, *Love's Coming of Age*, exploring marriage, gender roles and sexuality, was the first non-medical book to examine aspects of the then controversial 'woman question'. Its frank presentation of sex as life-enhancing was a startlingly new and bold outlook, but one that would open him to attack for undermining marriage and the family.

What makes him lastingly important is also the place that he occupies in the history of sexual *modernism* and its underlying theme of emancipation, which carried a number of distinct meanings for him. Most importantly, it meant the regeneration of sexual ideals: the overcoming of the idea of sex as something covert and shameful, covered and concealed by religious hypocrisy, while being bought and sold as a commodity. It meant the acceptance of sexual fulfilment as a primary need, essential to human well-being. It also meant a degree of sexual freedom, but not of licence. For lovers of their own sex, it meant the acceptance of their natures and the overcoming of the shame and guilt that blighted the lives of so many. Finally, once attitudes were open and sane, society might be emancipated *from* sex, and come to see it as only a part of the totality of human love.

In 1893, while writing the pamphlets that made up *Love's Coming of Age*, he was also preparing a daring pamphlet on homosexuality: *Homogenic Love and its Place in a Free Society*. Publications on homosexuality that circulated freely on the European continent were hardly known in England, where apart from its occasional mention in medical journals anything written on the subject was liable to be prosecuted for obscenity. In such a hostile environment the pamphlet, although initially printed for private circulation, was an unequivocal assault on the Victorian anti-homosexual dogma. Only months after its publication Oscar Wilde was imprisoned for gross indecency and a vicious assault was mounted by the English press on 'sexual deviants'. Refusing to bow in the face of such condemnation, Carpenter embarked on a decade-long defence of homosexuality, culminating in 1908 with the publication of *The Intermediate Sex*, the first publicly available book to appear in England defending homosexual relationships between consenting adults in private.

If the most important individual, Carpenter was not alone in confronting Victorian sexual codes. Two other men, John Addington Symonds and Havelock Ellis, also entered the field of sexual reform at this time and collaborated with Carpenter. Symonds, a leading literary critic, had written and privately circulated two monographs on homosexuality and wanted to make them more widely available. Ellis, a physician and editor of a series of books on scientific subjects, was also preparing to undertake a comprehensive study of human sexual psychology. When Symonds approached him with a proposal for a book combining his two monographs, the cautious Ellis considered that the subject of homosexuality was too risky for his series. Symonds then proposed that they should jointly author a book, suggesting that his historical and ethnological writing on homosexuality would fit well with material that Ellis could provide on the psychology of homosexuality. Ellis afterwards claimed that he had not intended to begin his studies with the subject of homosexuality but changed his mind after discovering, soon after his marriage to Edith Lees, that she was attracted to women. In a lengthy correspondence, the pair worked out the details for the book, but before they could meet to discuss it, Symonds died.

Ellis could have abandoned the project but Carpenter encouraged him to continue. Ellis then combined material from Symonds's work with his own research, and in 1896 and 1897 published it, firstly in German and then in English, with the title *Sexual Inversion*, a term then used to describe homosexuality. Although the book was principally a scientific examination, not a defence of homosexuality, it was seized by the police and prosecuted as an 'obscene libel'. Given the historical significance of this book, and Carpenter's close involvement in its writing, it forms an important part of this narrative.

Carpenter began his defence of homosexuality from a scientifically credible, if contested, position that it was innate, not a perversion or pathological condition. He took from the growing scientific literature on homosexuality facts that supported his own arguments, derived from self-knowledge and experience of everyday homosexual life. The claim that homosexuality was a morbid condition, which first arose from the study of inmates of prisons and mental institutions, was already being contested by the inclusion in the literature of a growing number of positive homosexual self-definitions. These autobiographical narratives formed a counter-discourse that challenged established medical theories and provided a foundation on which Carpenter built his case. He also drew on history and ethnology, to show the prevalence and acceptance of homosexuality across cultures; as counterpoints to a purely scientific understanding of the subject.

His tortuous journey from self-repression to acceptance of his sexual nature began, at a time of intense emotional fragility, with his discovery of the iconoclastic American poet Walt Whitman. In fear of the rigid social and legal taboos against the physical expression of his homosexuality, he had assumed a romanticised form of man-loving. Whitman's homoerotic poems, at last, sanctioned the expression of his sexual nature. More importantly, the empowerment to write about homosexuality flowed directly from Whitman. He later found it difficult to imagine what his life would have been like had he not come across the man who was to have a pivotal influence on the English homosexual fraternity. Whitman's homoerotic *Calamus* poems were seen as unmistakeably poetry of the body, and of the male body alone. For Carpenter, as with others, they were liberating.

His formative years were lived during a dynamic transitional period of English history. Five years before he went up to Cambridge two seminal works appeared that marked a sea-change for many Victorian intellectuals: Charles Darwin's *On the Origin of Species* and John Stuart Mill's *On Liberty*; the first challenging the biblical foundations of Christian belief, the second, in proposing a new definition of personal freedom, the Victorians' sense of social order. Carpenter, by now ordained into the Anglican Church and a Fellow of Trinity Hall, Cambridge, was caught up in the intense debates that these works spawned. At the same time, the more humane political economy of advanced liberals, men such as his tutor and family friend Henry

Fawcett, the republicanism that gripped the university in the early 1870s, and the Christian socialism of Frederick Denison Maurice, whose curate he was briefly, all shaped his development as a radical thinker.

In 1873, he experienced a damascene moment. Convinced that the unforgivable sin was infidelity to self, he abandoned the priesthood and his college fellowship for a life as an itinerant lecturer in the northern towns of England. The cottage that he had built on the edge of the Derbyshire Dales became part of his physical and mental recuperation; a powerful antidote to the suffocating artificiality of his life at Brighton and Cambridge. He trenched his seven acres, pruned his trees and took his produce to market; not as an act of rural self-sufficiency fashionable in his day among those seeking an escape from an urban existence, but as his chosen mode of living. He did it, like much else in his life, as he would say, to 'please myself'. But he had not broken away from his origins to become a recluse, content with his books to dream away his days. In his reaction against the modern world there was certainly more than a tinge of romantic nostalgia for what had been lost, and much utopian optimism, but he would grapple always with the here and now. It was the here and now that he wished to see humanised.

His involvement in having left Cambridge, his English radical politics began with the publication in 1883 of an idiosyncratic long prose poem, *Towards Democracy*; an excoriating critique of commercialism and the worst excesses of industrial capitalism. It was also a psychological history, an account of personal catharsis; of the release of long-suppressed feelings about both his homosexuality and the 'civilisation' exemplified by the family into which he had been born. It was the prelude to the most significant phase in his intellectual and personal development; his emotional life and movement towards the articulation of a critical sexual politics. The 1880s saw a new phase in working-class agitation, with demands for a living wage, increased union representation and parliamentary and franchise reforms. Recurrent large-scale unemployment and widespread poverty pricked consciences; drawing into political activity middle-class individuals like Carpenter, who formed a new intelligentsia morally repelled by the spectacle of brutalising work, social fragmentation and the spoliation of the environment.

His search for personal and sexual liberation also took place during the formative years of the British socialist movement. He was a prominent member of its intellectual vanguard and, although never a joiner, the many groups through which the movement was fashioned – the Fellowship of the New Life, the Social Democratic Federation, the Fabian Society, the Socialist League, Labour Churches, and the Independent Labour Party – were all ones to which he had some form of allegiance. But his linking of socialism with a vision of a new sexual culture, and his claims for the *naturalness* of same-sex attachments, alarmed many of the socialist movement's early pioneers. He also lost friends in the scientific community by rejecting Darwinism and espousing a theory of evolution based on *internal* development.

Although he devoted much time and energy to promoting the socialist cause, he was often disparaged for both his ideas and his faddish lifestyle. The socialist peacock George Bernard Shaw characterised him as the Noble Savage; the 'ultra-civilised impostor', the gentleman-scholar fortunate enough to possess the financial resources that enabled him to escape both the fatuity of bourgeois existence and the horrors of industrial life.

He did not make any lasting contribution to the advancement of socialist theory. He was an eclectic, able to unite the English Chartists' and Owenite heritage with the political economy of both John Stuart Mill and Karl Marx. But, on his death, he was widely regarded as one of the English socialist movement's spiritual fathers. He had caught the tide of his day: his two most popular and widely read political tracts, *England's Ideal* and *Civilisation: Its Cause and Cure*, appeared during this millenarian period of socialist formation, and at a time when there was a paucity of indigenous socialist literature. In numerous incidental publications and countless lectures and speeches spanning thirty years, travelling the length and breadth of Britain, filling large halls to overflowing, he argued unceasingly for fundamental changes to the industrial system and the distribution of power and wealth. His socialism was, at bottom, deeply ethical and based on the imperative of changing individuals' behaviour.

Importantly, his politics was always inextricably entwined with his struggle for self-validation, an extension of his critique of the sexual oppression of the Victorian bourgeoisie that had scarred his youth and early manhood. His belief in the social worth of the homosexual formed a bridge between his ideas on sexuality and his socialist convictions. He ventured to ask whether Eros could be a social leveller; whether 'comrade-alliance' could become a positive social force drawing members of different classes together, even forming the basis of a socialist brotherhood and a true democracy. It was Whitman's espousal of the social function of 'intense and loving comradeship', of the personal and passionate attachment of man to man, that had propelled him out of the Anglican church and his donnish existence into the mainstream of English working-class life.

When he entered the world of progressive politics there was little to distinguish his aspirations from those of his fellow socialists. This changed decisively in 1886, when he came to know the female emancipationist Olive Schreiner, who had arrived in England in 1883 from the then Cape Province. Their mutual attraction was immediate and intense and Carpenter was soon 'my Dear Boy'. She became the most significant influence on his personal life; a woman who understood his anguish when his first real love affair collapsed. Their friendship opened the most important chapter in his life, when he turned from writing on conventional socialist subjects to specific problems surrounding relationships between the sexes, and at a deeper level the modes of expression of the sexual instinct. In a society in which women were subordinated, Schreiner sought out men who would treat her as an equal; a collaborator, a fellow-worker. She found such a man in Carpenter and became the driving force behind his decision to write his women-related pamphlets.

His interests were wide-ranging, which has made him an unavoidable figure for historians of the late-Victorian era. But his talent for forging connections between quite diverse intellectual streams of thought was at the expense of over-all coherence. Only his writing on sexuality possesses the unity that makes its detachment from his wider work possible. Although the outlines of his sexual politics have been well documented in works on Victorian sexual ideology and practice, he has, for too long, been confined to the academic 'closet'. Exceptionally, Sheila Rowbotham's outstanding biography, *Edward Carpenter, A Life of Liberty and Love*, has finally brought him into the everyday world.

Here, we combine scholarship with accessibility, for the reader who is interested in understanding Carpenter's life as a gay man, his place in the history of English homosexual liberation and his seminal writing on sex. Using a large number of previously unpublished letters to his lovers, friends and fellow-socialists, his tortuous journey from conforming youth to outspoken critic of Victorian society is traced. His adolescent hurts and sexual confusion; his fumbling first love affairs and the remarkable expansion of his mind at Cambridge are recounted, together with his fortuitous escape from a priestly and donnish life. His entry into the world of socialist politics as a radical and polemical writer, and his turning from socialist rhetoric to sexual politics forms a central part of this narrative; together with his struggle to find publishers daring enough to take his books at the height of the Wilde scandals. Exceptionally, for the first time, the intimate details of his gay life are combined with an extensive analysis of his pioneering texts on homosexuality.

PART ONE

1

A House of Mammon

Descended from a distinguished naval family, Charles Carpenter had followed his own father into the service at the tender age of thirteen. Being introspective and studious, it was a life to which he was entirely unsuited: a life only made tolerable during the long periods of idleness at sea by learning German and devouring philosophical works. In time, the combination of a rough monotonous life and the hazards of armed skirmishes affected his health, and at the age of twenty-five he found himself a landlubber without a profession. Encouraged by his father, he turned to the law and at the late age of thirty-two was called to the English Bar and began a practice in Chancery. In 1833, he married Sophia Wilson, the daughter of Thomas Wilson, a blunt-speaking Scot who had also been a naval man. A widower, for his comfort, he agreed to the marriage on the condition that the couple lived with him at Walthamstow, a sleepy Essex village on the edge of Epping Forest.

Living a considerable distance from the London law courts was not practicable, but he made the best of his situation and

3

worked for several years to establish himself, although it was clear that temperamentally he was as ill-suited to the Bar as he had been to the foredeck. With a young family increasing year by year, a wife tied firmly to a demanding father's coat-tails, and briefs to be mastered, his health suddenly collapsed. For the second time, he was forced to give up a profession, leaving the family bereft of a regular income. It was not until Thomas Wilson's death that a change in the family's circumstances became possible and in 1842 they left London for Brighton on the English south coast, then a fashionable resort for London's wealthy. Their new home in Brunswick Square within sight of the seashore, with a warren of rooms and staircases, was soon echoing to the boisterous shouts and scampering feet of the Carpenter brood. Edward, the third of four boys and a brother to six sisters, was brought into the world on the 29th of August 1844.

After his virtual entombment in London, the more congenial surroundings of Brighton might have led to an improvement in Charles Carpenter's state of mind, but the change did little to mend matters. His financial position was insecure and having sole responsibility for his family's well-being made him anxious and restless. The first two or three years in Brighton, Edward's mother would tell him, were the worst in his parents' married life. It was not until his father's death, when he came into a substantial inheritance, that there was a marked change in the family's financial circumstances. But one worry was replaced by another, for now the family's well-being rested upon his acumen in managing his assets. The ever-present prospect of the family being reduced to penury as a result of his financial incompetence would haunt him for years and induce periodic fits of intense nervousness. When Edward, in turn, was plagued by his own mental demons he would recall his father telling him, 'it is not labour but anxiety that kills'. It was one of the symptoms of a malady to which the Victorians had long since given the clinical description *neurasthenia*: an ailment of the restless bourgeoisie more than any other social strata. As it was often put down to heredity, the ever-anxious Edward may have come to believe that he too was cursed by it.

Given his decision not to return to the Bar there was an inevitability about the future that lay before Charles Carpenter. His life would have to be that of the respectable *rentier* and the aims and ideals of this class would have to become his own. It was in this role that his father's life would be fixed in the young Edward's mind. It was the life of a man under the constant stress of sustaining the family's financial security and social respectability. It consumed his waking hours: as markets rose and fell, he worried excessively about his ability to leave his unmarried girls an income. There were many times when even his books failed to save him from despondent days and sleepless nights brought on by some failure among his investments. On such occasions, he would appear at the breakfast table looking a picture of misery and declare that the girls would have to 'go out as governesses'. Silence and gloom would descend on the household until stocks picked up, after which the domestic panic would subside and the usual life of dinner parties and balls would be resumed. Edward's close observation of the day-to-day lives of his sisters would deeply influence his ideas about the opposite sex and would make him a committed advocate of female equality. They were denied education outside the home, and raised with the single-minded purpose of making a good marriage. He saw the life of the middle-class young lady of his day as 'tragic in its emptiness'. Apart from social engagements and promenading, only literary and musical cultivation could provide an outlet for his sisters' energies.

Most significantly for his future life, he learned at first-hand what it meant to belong to the *rentier* class. As he would write in his autobiographical notes:

> Coming to my first consciousness, as it were, of the world at
> the age of sixteen … I found myself – and without knowing

where I was – in the middle of that strange period of human evolution, the Victoria Age, which in some respects, one now thinks, marked the lowest ebb of modern civilised society: a period in which not only commercialism in public life, but cant in religion, pure materialism in science, futility in social conventions, the worship of stocks and shares, the starving of the human heart, the denial of the human body and its needs, the huddling concealment of the body in clothes, the "impure hush" on matters of sex, class division, contempt of manual labour, and the cruel barring of women from every natural and useful expression of their lives, were carried to an extremity of folly difficult for us now to realize.[1]

His two elder brothers had already left home and whenever a potential financial crisis loomed, he would be called upon to assist with his father's investigations. Reports of railway companies, newspaper cuttings and other carefully accumulated items would be got out and pored over. He would frequently have to sit up till the small hours sharing his father's painful suspense. Although he would afterwards make light of these occasions, when he was 'put in the stocks', the experience left more than a passing impression. Over time, it nurtured a seed of 'unexpressed hatred' for the social conditions into which he had been born; for a way of life supported by the toil of others; of domestic servants, farm labourers and artisans in far-distant manufacturing towns. He would later write: 'What cares, what anxieties, what yellow and blue fits, what sleepless nights, dance attendance on the worshipper in the great temple of Stocks! The capricious deity that dwells there has to be appeased by ceaseless offerings'.[2] He was aware that he belonged to a class for which financial return was everything; a class, which living off its rents, interest and dividends, cultivated a life of ostentatious contentment, polite manners and assumed social superiority; a class with its face 'turned away from the wriggling poverty that made it rich'.[3]

The fusing of the commercial mentality with gentility was exemplified in everyday family life, but Edward's head would always be in conflict with his heart. His parents could not 'fly out of the conditions in which they belonged'. They, too, were prisoners of the commercial system; as much victims, in his eyes, as the multitude of anonymous individuals whose life-destroying toil was the price to be paid for their ease. Later, when he was most contemptuous of the 'sickly white hands of idleness', of, in his eyes, this *dehumanised* class, his piety demanded that he should work for the deliverance of his parents' kind.

Charles Carpenter's life had become one of compromise and hidden disappointments. It was a life 'as broad as it could well be upon the foundation of that particular social status to which he belonged',[4] and for his family's sake he reconciled himself to the humdrum conventionalities of his social position, doing good work as a Brighton magistrate. It was fortunate that he was a man of culture with a rich interior life that removed him spiritually from the money-grubbing aims that consumed the society around him. He did not have a study, being content to read in the drawing room, seemingly indifferent to the tumult of the children's wild games. He would frequently sit up until the early hours poring over a new book or re-reading passages from the works of his favourite philosophers. One of Edward's most vivid memories of his early life would be of the whole family gathered in the drawing room after dinner. His mother might sow, his sisters might play the piano or sing a little, but the main family activity was reading:

> My father would get out his Fichte, or his Hartmann and soon become lost in their perusal. Occasionally he would, when he came to a striking passage, play a sort of devil's tattoo with his fingers on the table, or, getting up, would walk to-and-fro quarter-deck fashion, with creaky boots, and reciting his authors to himself. Then my mother or perhaps my eldest

sister would remonstrate, and after a time he would settle down again. Sometimes, if he was very quiet one might look up from one's book and see from his upturned eyes and half-open lips that he had lapsed into inner communion and meditation.[5]

Given his benign father and devoted, if distant, mother, it is puzzling that he was to declare that he was not a happy child; that at home, he 'never felt really at home'. 'It may seem ungrateful to say so, but my abiding recollection of my early days is one of discomfort'.[6] Lapped in the attentive services of a well-to-do household and raised to a life of privilege surrounded by servants, he had a hundred advantages denied to an ordinary 'child of the people', but from an early age he experienced a deep sense of emotional and social maladjustment; of unhappiness with himself and his class:

> The social life which encircled us in Brighton was artificial enough; but it was the standard which we children had to live to ... I hated the life, was miserable in it – the heartless conventionalities, silly proprieties – but I never imagined, it never occurred to me, that there *was* any other life. To be pursued by the dread of appearances – what people would say about one's clothes or one's speech – to be always in fear of committing unconscious trespasses of invisible rules – this seemed in my childhood the normal condition of existence; so much so that I never dreamed of escaping from it. I only prayed for a time when grace might be given me to pass by without reproach.[7]

Such an early detachment from his class is not easily explained. A niece recalled that the Carpenters were 'not disposed to question or despise their milieu. They were ready to get the best out of life as they found it, and they absorbed current ideas with facility', adding, 'No brood could have seemed less likely to hatch a revolutionary.'[8] We should guard against a crude reductionism; whereby much of what he later did and wrote can be interpreted as a reaction against childhood loneliness or adolescent hurts. But his scathing denials of the worthiness of the class that had nurtured him would be expressed in language not heard since Carlyle. His parents, despite their conventional emotional distance from their children, would appear blameless. In the upper echelons, Victorian family life is often depicted as one presided over by an authoritarian *pater familias* ruling with a subservient wife over sat-upon children. Edward suffered no such fate at the hands of his own kindly father, with his benign indifference to domestic life, lost in his books and reveries. He was an Anglican of the 'broad church' persuasion, liberal and eclectic, and the forbearance that followed from his religious beliefs spared Edward from the crippling of the spirit that other prominent Victorians were to recall in accounts of their childhoods.[9]

In adolescence he sought consolation by closeness to the wild untamed elements of the sea and nearby downs. He would sit on the beach and dream, and fifty years later, 'sit on the shore of human life and dream practically the same dreams'.[10] Nature then meant more to him 'than any human attachment'.[11] The downs became his favourite refuge. On sunny days he would wander alone for miles, with brooding, ill-defined, half-shaped thoughts. It was a world remote from habitations, with only the occasional shepherd to be seen huddled in his cloak; where he could lie up for hours in a secluded hollow, eyes fixed dreamily on the great ragged clouds careering above. On other days, horse-riding over the downs with a favourite sister always raised his spirits.

Although 45 Brunswick Square was a house in which there was much laughter and a great deal of unruly fun, his mother found open manifestations of feeling unbecoming. This reserve, ingrained in her youth, had in adulthood become involuntary. For Edward, childhood and adolescence was a time of emotional concealment, a covered underground life. The description of his character penned in his autobiographical notes is one of self-deprecation; of a timid, unduly sensitive, conforming boy; never daring, with a spirit 'sadly lacking in the inestimable virtue of revolt'. He felt himself to be 'an alien, an outcast, a failure and an object of ridicule'.[12]

Looking back, he could not recall a single occasion, until he was nineteen or twenty, when, if troubled or perplexed, he was able to go to anyone for consolation. Children were taught early in life that their thoughts and feelings were not intended to be dissected for the benefit of others. For boys, such emotional suppression was frequently justified as a kind of training for adulthood; as a foundation for *manliness*, the quintessential Victorian ideal.

The interdict against demonstrative affection had early been brought home sharply to John Addington Symonds. On his twelfth birthday he went up to kiss his father, only to be rebuffed: 'Shake hands; you are growing too old for kissing'. He felt ashamed of having offered what had been rendered unseemly and took a step upon the path towards isolation. '[There] was something savage in me which accepted the remark with approval. Henceforth I shrank from the exposure of emotion, except upon paper, in letters and in studied language'.[13]

Edward's parents left him to fathom the mysteries of his sexual awakening. He traced his desire for a 'passionate attachment' to a member of his own sex to his earliest boyhood. Long before any distinct sexual feelings declared themselves, he felt a friendly attraction towards other boys:

> I worshipped the very ground on which some, generally elder, boys stood; they were heroes for whom I would have done anything. I dreamed about them at night, absorbed them with my eyes in the day, watched them at cricket, loved to press against them unnoticed in a football melly, or even to get accidentally hurt by one of them at hockey, was glad if they just

spoke to me or smiled; but never got a word further with it all. What could I say?[14]

As a day-boy at Brighton College he was not caught up in the sexual fumblings found in the boarders' dormitory. For John Addington Symonds, the combination of brutality and lust that he found at Harrow made him fear that he had stumbled into the land of Swift's Yahoos. Like Edward, his own erotic day-dreaming about boys seemed to belong to another world:

> Every boy of good looks had a female name, and was recognized either as a public prostitute or as some bigger fellow's 'bitch'. Bitch was the word in common usage to indicate a boy who yielded his person to a lover. The talk in the dormitories and the studies was incredibly obscene. Here and there one could not avoid seeing acts of onanism, mutual masturbation, and the sports of naked boys in bed together. There was no refinement, no sentiment, no passion; nothing but animal lust in these occurrences.[15]

Without such experiences, Edward's passion for his own sex developed itself gradually, utterly uninfluenced from the outside. 'I never even, during all this period, and till a good deal later, learned the practice of masturbation'.[16] It spared him the feelings of guilt, even wickedness, that the constant strictures against 'self-abuse' could induce. The Victorians' obsession with controlling any form of non-procreative sex made the masturbator a kind of archetypal deviant.

His blissful ignorance of youthful sexual behaviour brought one blessing, for no sense of shame or repulsion about sexual acts seemed to have become implanted in his mind. When this realm of life was finally opened up to him, he regarded sex as perfectly natural, 'like digestion' or any other bodily function. He did not have to root out a deep-seated incubus of shame before he could write frankly about sex. But, despite his lack of homosexual experience, there was little doubt where his erotic interests lay. By the time he reached sexual maturity, the female attractions then set before the eyes of young men, whether 'hapless young ladyisms' or the 'beauties of the gutter', were 'a detestable boredom'.[17]

At about the age of fourteen, the sight of a smooth-haired carefully shaven young curate in his spotless surplice must have given him a fatal bias towards religion, for it entered his mind that he would like to become a clergyman. Without any prompting, he assumed an intense piousness. When, already nineteen, he left Brighton College his future had still not been decided. He had developed an interest in science, conducting small experiments with some chemical apparatus left behind by his eldest brother. Making a connection between chemicals and medicine led him to think quite seriously about being a doctor, although he was still 'inclined to go into Orders'.[18] Charles Carpenter, resisting his son's wish, decided to send him off to Heidelberg for six months to acquire some German and attend a few classes at the university. He took lodgings in a professor's house and was soon writing home to let everybody know that he was not fighting duels. But his religious earnestness persisted, and on Sundays, prim and proper, he would march off to the English church wearing a tall hat.

By now, he had decided that he wished to go to Cambridge and was soon fretting about his future. In a surprisingly assertive letter, he broached the matter with his father:

> I am beginning to have an idea of speaking [German] coherently, and it is time I should as I have already, I suppose, been half my time here, that is; if I go to Cambridge in October; I suppose you have not yet put down my name ... If you intend that I should go it is quite time to do so; if not please write soon and tell me, as it is no use delaying.[19]

Little over a week later he returned to the subject, his father having now agreed that he could go to Cambridge, but not to Trinity Hall, the college of his choice: 'I thought we had quite decided that Trinity should be my college. I do not wish to go to St John's; and I do not think that the chance of my distinguishing myself in a large college is sufficiently good to make me throw up the advantages of Trinity, in the way of friends, teaching and so on.' Concerned that his father's indecisiveness might lead to his missing entry that year, he implored him to find out the date by which he had to be entered for the college, and the subjects required for matriculation.[20]

Arriving back in Brighton, he alarmed the family with talk of training for holy orders immediately. A compromise was reached: he could go to Cambridge to read classics, and, although his older brother Charlie advised his father that the Church would be 'a suitable profession' for him, he should not be allowed to take orders for some time. Knowing how narrow and sheltered his brother's life had been, he suggested that he needed to 'acquire all possible experience, to see as much of all kinds of classes of people as he possibly can before entering the Church … Unless he has acquired experience and knowledge of the world beforehand, I think there is a danger of his becoming narrow minded and illiberal afterwards'.[21] Relieved that his son's immediate entry to the Church had been averted, his father yielded to his wish to enter Trinity Hall.

2

The Awakening

In the autumn of 1864, he went up to Trinity Hall. The college had long been the preserve of lawyers, and Charles Carpenter, even at this stage, may have hoped that law and not the Church would be his son's eventual profession. He soon found himself in the thick of the rowing set. Even 'intellectually strenuous' young men were to be found on the river and not to row or help in some other way was considered to be a kind of apostasy. The lean, athletic 'Chips' was made stroke of the college's second boat. He became secretary of the boat club, talked boating slang and for two years wore out the seat of his breeches with incessant aquatic service.

Rowing soon became entwined with romance. The close physical contact with healthy muscular companions eased his yearning but male demonstrations of affection were foreclosed. Fear of revelation, disgrace, and ostracism or worse forced those with his feelings to sublimate or conquer them. The secret of his longing was locked up inside. Pretence became a way of life, which in the closed society of a college was suffocating. His eyes absorbed, his imagination invented, but the voice was mute. 'I consumed my own smoke' was how he would describe his unspoken infatuations.[1]

'This succession of athletic and even beautiful faces and figures, what a strange magnetism they had for me, and yet all the while how insurmountable for the most part was the barrier between'.[2] He was haunted by 'ideal visions and incomplete romances', for which in the daylight world there seemed to be no place. Confused by his emotions, he even asked himself: 'Was I really a woman born in some inner unknown region of my nature'?[3]

As he moved daily among 'gilded and silvered youths' the realisation of the strength of his emotional and physical needs increased his personal anguish. 'Of what avail was the brain, when the heart demanded so much, and demanding was still unsatisfied'?[4] His self-repressive education, his reserved habits, the fatuities of public opinion, all conspired to seal his lips: '[I] did not give myself the utterance I ought to have given. By concealing myself I was unfair to my friends, and at the same time suffered torments which I need not have suffered'.[5]

Years later, on returning to Trinity Hall, he relived his inner tumult and the longings that had occupied the whole background of his life: 'The figures and faces of friends poignant with what attractions, filling one with passions one dared not speak, faintly reciprocated'.[6]

And he would later write:

It is difficult … for outsiders not personally experienced in the matter to realise the great strain and tension of nerves under which those persons grow up from boyhood to manhood … who find their deepest and strongest instincts under the ban of the society around them; who before they clearly understand the drift of their own nature discover that they are somehow cut off from the sympathy and understanding of those nearest to them; and who know that they can never give expression to their tenderest yearnings of affection without exposing themselves to the possible charge of actions stigmatised as odious crimes.[7]

Before he arrived, he had imagined everyone would talk Latin and he, lamely taught at school and coming late from loafing in Germany, would struggle to make any kind of mark. But he had a flair for mathematics, and after coming first in a college examination decided to take his degree in the subject. But, mathematics apart, his interests were rapidly broadening into new fields. In his second year he was awarded a college prize for a very self-defining essay, *On the Continuance of Modern Civilisation*. It was an elegantly written appraisal of the danger of an over-powerful state potentially suppressing personal liberty; a deleterious commercialism; class divisions and extremes of wealth and poverty. In no country, he wrote, was 'class domination and class interest so extensive, and the contrast between wealth and poverty so visible'. His treatment of 'commercialism' was clearly that of the son of a *rentier* reliving 'the anxieties inherent in a life spent in such pursuit'. There was a further statement of real significance for the future. Science was not omniscient. 'We are like men passing by a Cathedral and faintly catching a few notes of some grand anthem played within'.[8] Nearly twenty years later he will shock his mathematical and scientific friends by describing modern science as only a stage in human understanding that had to be passed through 'on the way to a higher order of perception or consciousness'.[9] The essay revealed the intellectual influences at work and may rightly be seen as the precursor of a powerful critique to come in his *Civilisation: Its Cause and Cure*.

In 1867 one of the College's clerical fellowships had been vacated by Leslie Stephen (father of Virginia Woolf and Vanessa Bell), who later confessed that he had 'taken orders, rashly'.[10] When sounded out, Edward affirmed that he still wished to be ordained and was practically offered the fellowship before sitting his final examinations. He was flattered to have been approached and wrote to his still sceptical father: 'I have just had a very good offer. I wish you would let me know what you think about it'. He was keen to point out the financial advantages, 'as besides holding a Lectureship and Fellowship, I should probably be able to take pupils, which is a profitable trade'. His emphasis on the material benefits of the fellowship was probably intended to offset his father's initial antipathy to his taking orders, by setting before him the prospect of the imminent removal of the financial burden of supporting him. 'The satisfaction of being able at last to turn to account all the money you have spent on my education is a great inducement to me to close with the offer at once', he wrote.[11]

Notwithstanding doubts about Edward entering the Church, the prospect of having a Cambridge fellow in the family was welcomed. His brother Charlie wrote playfully from India: 'How big are you? I want to have you here just for five minutes. Either to punch your head or let you punch mine. It would even relieve me to throw something at you. I am immensely pleased to hear of you having a Fellowship offered to you'.[12]

Brought up in the philosophical 'broad churchism' of his father with its seemingly ever-expanding horizon, he harboured no sense of antagonism to the Church and its teachings. He imagined it widening and growing from within, adapting to the times, particularly to the new thinking that the impact of contemporary scientific discoveries demanded. But when it came to doctrinal matters, he hardly appreciated how far he had drifted; as a skirmish with the bishop who would ordain him would reveal. He was a beneficiary of the tolerant theological climate in the Anglican Communion: it was important to be a *sincere* believer, but the actual beliefs demanded were the least dogmatic and capable of the widest interpretation. And the absence of religious conflicts at Cambridge at this time, unlike at Oxford, meant that a person with his questionable beliefs was relatively safe. Yet it was not his heterodox religious beliefs that worried him but the prospect of a university existence.

> I have always thought that the life of a Don is rather a stagnant sort of life and I do not think I could make up my mind to settle down altogether as such. At the same time, I do not think that I ought to refuse such a good opening, because even if I do remain here altogether, it will be very likely to lead to something else, and a few years spent here would not have been wasted.[13]

In 1868, at the age of twenty-four, he gained a first-class degree in the mathematical tripos; more than sufficient for a college fellowship. Notably, he was still attracting attention outside of mathematics, for shortly after graduating he was awarded the university's prestigious Burney Prize of £100 for a heavily Ruskinian essay on *The Religious Influence of Art*. Its subtitle was 'The Legitimate Province of Architecture, Painting and Music in the Service of Religion'. That he could write on such a High Church topic (the Oxford movement had sought to restore the place of the aesthetic in worship) is a significant pointer to the fluid state of his mind. It became his first formal publication.[14]

Relaxing that summer, his future seemingly secure, he was handed a little blue book of poems by the American writer Walt Whitman, edited by his English admirer William Michael Rossetti.[15] Rossetti wanted this iconoclastic voice from the New World to be heard in England; hoping that, like a stone dropped into a pond, its influence might 'spread out its concentric circles of consequences'. With a free hand, but aware that the 'audacities of topic and of expression' to be found in Whitman might alarm refined English readers, he left out every poem that he judged could be considered 'offensive to the feeling of morals or propriety in this peculiarly nervous age'. He pointed to the 'indecencies' scattered throughout the poems, although he felt to call them immoralities would be going too far. They were 'deforming crudities', raw and ugly, on the ground of poetic or literary art.[16]

In America, there were those who had no doubt that many of Whitman's poems celebrated love between men, and condemned him out of hand as immoral. Others wanted to recognise Whitman as a highly innovative poet but were unable to countenance a homosexual content and read such poems metaphorically as depictions of ideal love, or of asexual friendship. They were unable to separate their response to his poetry from their moralistic attitudes towards homosexuality.

Carpenter would not have been one of the 'consequences' anticipated by Rossetti. It was only by chance that he had discovered the utterances of the individual who was destined to influence the whole course of his life. Whitman's overpowering presence in his poems mesmerised him. He saw that, cast in literature, was a complete man, with all his pride and passion; encompassing the whole gamut of human experience from end to end, with all its harmonies and discords, nothing concealed.

Whitman's poetry was about bonding of the most sensuous kind and Carpenter was electrified by the poems that celebrated *comradeship*: 'That thought, so near and personal to me, I had never before seen or heard fairly expressed, even in Plato and the Greek authors there had been something wanting'.[17] At last, and 'with a great leap of joy', he had found the treatment of sex 'which accorded with my own sentiments'.[18]

The editor's judicious selection had failed to exclude a number of homoerotic poems clearly addressed to men; poems that spoke in natural, undisguised language of everyday fleeting encounters with men who caught and responded to Whitman's roving eye, as in 'To A Stranger'. Carpenter could not have missed its overt homosexuality:

Passing stranger! You do not know how longingly
I look upon you …

> You give me the pleasure of your eyes, face, flesh, as we
> pass – you take of my beard, breast, hands,
> In return,
> I am not to speak to you – I am to think of you when I
> sit alone, or wake at night alone,
> I am to wait – I do not doubt I am to meet you again,
> I am to see to it that I do not lose you.

And 'Among the Multitude':

> Among the men and women, the multitude,
> I perceive one picking me out by secret and divine signs;
> Acknowledging none else – not parent, wife, husband,
> brother, child, any nearer than I am;
> Some are baffled. – But that one is not – that one knows me
> Ah, lover and perfect equal!
> I meant that you should discover me so, by my faint indirections;
> And I, when I meet you, mean to discover you by the like in
> you.[19]

The poet's dominating personality shone so clearly through his writing that he was aware, if only dimly at first, that he had come into contact with, if not great thoughts or theories, a great life *lived*; a life celebrated. As he learned more about Whitman's life it magnified his own ensnarement by the 'intellectual furniture' that so constrained the expression of his own nature. By example, Whitman had shown that what was all-important was 'character and the statement of Self'.[20] This single precept would come to shape Carpenter's life; would be the general rule by which he would live. Individuals able to 'express or liberate their *own* real and deep-rooted needs and feelings', he would say towards the end of his life, could, as Whitman had for him, 'liberate and aid the expression of the lives of thousands of others'. Whitman had revealed to him his inexorable destiny for, if by following

Whitman, he had himself been such an exemplar, he could claim no credit for 'what a man does out of the necessity of his nature'.[21]

He soon acquired his own copy, reading the poems over and over again, finding an 'inexhaustible quality and power of making me return to them'.[22] On long summer nights in the college garden or beside the Cam, he would feel his life flowing away from his surroundings, carried on a current of sympathy westward across the Atlantic. For the first time, he felt connected to a person giving voice to his own inner feelings. Whitman had written in the poem *Other Lands:*

> This moment yearning and thoughtful, sitting alone,
> It seems to me there are other men in other lands,
> Yearning and thoughtful;
> And it seems to me if I could know those men I should
> become attached to them, as I do to men in my
> own lands,
> Oh I know we should be brethren and lovers,
> I know I should be happy with them. [23]

Following his discovery of Whitman's poetry, he had acquired a copy of his *Democratic Vistas*. If *Leaves of Grass* awakened his suppressed sexuality, it was Whitman's critical review of the deficiencies of post–Civil War American nationhood that helped to give shape to his politics. He took as much from this long essay, full of passion and verve, as he will take from any of the political and economic tracts that underpinned English radicalism of the 1880s. *Democratic Vistas* was 'a mine of new thoughts'; a powerful political manifesto. Here was an idea of democracy that was not about constitutions, or institutions, or popular enfranchisement:

> We have frequently printed the word Democracy. Yet I cannot
> too often repeat that it is a word the real gist of which still
> sleeps, quite unawakened, notwithstanding the resonance and

the many angry tempests out of which its syllables have come, from pen or tongue it is a great word whose history, I suppose, remains unwritten, because that history is yet to be enacted.[24]

Carpenter would write later: 'As the ideal of the Feudal Age was upheld and presented to the world in its great poetry, so the new ideal of the Democratic Age will be upheld and presented to the world in the great poetry of Democracy'.[25] He read *Democratic Vistas* and the little blue book of poems over and over again, finding an 'inexhaustible quality and power of making me return to them'.[26]

Reading Whitman eased his emotional longings but did not lead to an immediate reshaping of his artistic ideals. He continued to exist in a kind of literary backwater, marooned on the shores of conventional prosody. There was still an imprisonment of the feelings and a stultification of poetic form. For several more years he would labour over the composition of orthodox verse, his artistic and emotional conceptions still ruled by his old masters, Shelley and Wordsworth. He struggled to perfect the customary techniques for handling words and rhythmical forms, whilst vaguely conscious that the high watermark of expression in rhyme and metre of this kind had long been reached. 'Nothing *more* perfect in that line could possibly be done', he would later write.[27] But he did not dare to leap into the ocean of metrical freedom that was Whitman. A dozen years would pass before, in *Towards Democracy*, he would break free from versifying that was merely 'composed' and write what was 'felt'.

In the autumn of 1868, he went into residence as a lecturer, was elected to the clerical fellowship and was admitted to the Church of England as a curate. He had been sleep-walking. Once immersed in ritualised worship he felt the reality, and the *unreality*, of the priesthood. He had to take services in the college chapel to an accompaniment of winks and grins from students, the shuffling of hassocks and the clicking of watches timing his performance on cold winter mornings. The gaping signs of unconcealed boredom on the faces of the somnolent dons was an added irritation.

He quickly sought a curacy at the nearby parish church of St Edwards, (in the gift of Trinity Hall), thinking to find there 'something more satisfactory and more definite in the way of Church work'.[28] But any sentiments that he harboured for the priesthood evaporated in the face of the deadly philistinism of the little provincial congregation of tradesmen and shopkeepers. An 'insuperable feeling of falsity' overcame him when he was required to stand up and recite the Creeds to a congregation that he believed did not understand a word.[29] Doubt now began to find its way into his sermons: 'If there is one thing certain in this world it is that it is better to be true than false. It does not matter whether truth leads you to be a Nonconformist or a Roman Catholic or anything else. It is a thousand times better to be a *true* Atheist than a *false* worshipper in the House of God'.[30] In the summer of 1870 he was ordained, but not before a doctrinal confrontation with the Bishop of Ely over some daring theological views, including a 'dreadful heresy' that he had rashly committed to paper. The equanimity with which he put this behind him; his apparent lack of concern that he was harbouring not just heterodox but heretical views, bore the stamp of the sentiments learned at his father's knee.

Ordination did little to reconcile him to his circumstances. Shortly afterwards, his equanimity was further disturbed when the St Edward's living became vacant. He was the obvious person to fill it, but he had by now come to dislike intensely a congregation used to boisterous hymns and evangelical sermons of the 'thunder and treacle' kind, against which his own calm, reflective offerings from the pulpit must have appeared dull. To 'write or sermonize any longer' for such a congregation was impossible, he told a fellow priest.[31] In the event, he did not have to decline the living, for early in 1871 the little flock acquired a most eminent shepherd in the form of Frederick Denison Maurice. He had been an undergraduate at Trinity Hall and was now the university's Professor of Moral Philosophy. He was renowned for being a very uncommon clergyman, holding radical views as a leader of the Christian Socialist movement. Initially, his presence raised Carpenter's spirits: 'I am so glad Maurice has brought an odour of Heaven to you – it is almost a necessity to have such an odour when one is surrounded by common-place skulls' wrote his sister Lizzie.[32] The saintly Maurice was the incarnation of earnestness and deeply human feeling but not of clear-headedness. His sermons did not help Carpenter to think straight about his own beliefs.

His ideas at this time were liberal, largely influenced by Henry Fawcett, family friend and Professor of Political Economy. He attended Fawcett's lectures on *continental* socialism and his arguments pervaded a number of his sermons. The working class, if controlled by demagogues, was a dangerous force, for 'this people is many, and ignorant, and passionate, confusing the good and evil together ... not very gentle when it rises in an angry flood to sweep away all alike'. It was important 'to keep the very possibility of such moments for ever from our shores'. However, it was clear where his sympathies lay. The socialists' schemes, 'formed hastily and under a sense of wrong', might be crude and impracticable but they were motivated by 'nobility of mind'.[33] There was significant support in England at this time for the Paris Commune, the radical socialist government that ruled Paris for two months in the spring of 1871. The University Republican Club was a hotbed, with a manifesto that expressed hostility to the hereditary principle exemplified by monarchical and aristocratic institutions. Carpenter occasionally attended meetings but did not join the club: the first instance of what would become a life-long practice of avoiding specific political allegiances. But he had already rehearsed his republican credentials in his essay on civilisation: 'The individual caprices of kings no longer give rise to monster Pyramids, or to works whose only office is to perpetuate the gigantic iniquity of the founder'.[34] But it is an indication of his shifting state of mind that at the same time as he was dabbling in arm-chair republicanism he was being considered for employment in the most august of spheres, as tutor to Queen Victoria's grandsons, the Princes George Frederick and Albert Victor. As Carpenter, perhaps to avoid embarrassment, never spoke or wrote about it, the circumstances under which the offer came about, and why it was not taken up, remain obscure. The post was eventually filled by his fellow priest and friend John Neale Dalton. It was a turning point in the lives of both men, 'one rising to spend his life with the highest in the land, the other choosing to live among the lowest'.[35]

It was during this time, that at one of the small university discussion societies he met Ponnambalam Arunachalam, a Christ Church undergraduate from a wealthy high-caste Ceylonese Tamil family. He was captivated by Ponnambalam's 'extraordinary quickness and receptiveness of mind', with 'some of the Tamil archness and bedevilment about him'. He must have found him physically appealing, for the form of the Tamil, 'mostly slight and graceful in figure', would entrance him when fifteen years later he visited him in Ceylon.[36] They may have discussed the erotic aspects of Hindu philosophy, at a time when he was grappling with sexual repression; even reached a level of intimacy that allowed him to, at least, hint at his sexuality. There would be much knowingness in Ponnambalam's subsequent long confessional letters to him. He would later send him an English translation of the great religious and philosophical Hindu poem, the *Bhagavad Gita*. It would open his mind to the sacred literature of the East, and act as a catalyst for the writing of *Towards Democracy*.

At the very time that he was battling with his religion, he became caught up in two conflicting romantic entanglements.

By May 1871, he felt so wretched that he begged off his lectures, and, in his own words, 'ran away' to Europe with Andrew Beck, a fellow Trinity Hall don.[37] Carpenter's recollections of his homosexual experiences at Cambridge are ambiguous. In the account of his sexual history given to Havelock Ellis, he wrote that his love for his own sex never found physical expression 'till I was fully twenty years of age'. The text runs on: 'I came to find that there were others like myself. I made a few special friends, and at last it came to me occasionally to sleep with them and to satisfy my imperious need for mutual embraces and emissions.'[38] But at the age of twenty he had scarcely settled in at Cambridge, where *all* his male friendships were to be marked, in his own words, by 'repressed passion and torment'. In an early draft of *My Days and Dreams*, he described his Cambridge friendships as being of 'a reserved abortive kind'. The romance that he hungered for 'never got itself expressed'.[39]

Letters that went to-and-fro at this time reveal a different picture: if there was no sex with Beck, for Carpenter there was certainly romance. Beck had come up to Cambridge at the same time and they went about together a good deal. Carpenter was his 'sunlit hemisphere', and more familiarly, his 'Tops'. Returning from a visit to the National Gallery, Beck recalled 'a great blurring of banners, my Ganymede, and all the Turners encausticised [*sic*] into one great burning line of sunset sea, all set in a halo of Edward'.[40] Beck, as a classicist, was well aware that Ganymede, the beautiful Trojan youth carried off by an eagle to be Zeus's cup-bearer, was a homosexual archetype.

They made a leisurely tour of Europe and being with Beck raised his spirits: 'We enjoyed ourselves enormously … we expatiated among the flowers and snow of Switzerland; and dreamed of symphonies of colour amid the Italian lakes; and melted with astonishment and heat in Milan; and lived a long time ago at Venice; and went up to heaven in an incense-cloud of art at Munich …'[41] The recipient of this missive was Charles

Oates, who was also a lover of his own sex. Their letters make the intimate nature of their friendship abundantly clear. After Oates made him a gift of a picture, Carpenter responded, 'I am sure you need not fear about it reminding me of you'.[42] And after receiving some poetic lines: 'Thank you a thousand times for sending me those lines. Sad as they make me feel in one sense, that you should have to have recourse to so poor a thing as the memory of me'.[43]

On his return to Brighton, he found a letter from Oates. It must have contained endearments, prompting Carpenter to respond: 'I feel that it is perhaps unfair – and indeed unsafe for me to take you in the same spirit now. You may have married. It makes me regret all the more that I did not write to you when I was abroad, as I often intended to do'.[44]

Only days earlier, Beck had abruptly drawn back from further intimacies with him. A too-close friendship might carry dangers for a clever country boy without connections; compromise his masculinity and impede his progress. It was time to distance himself from his *Ganymede*:

> You have no idea how practical I am. Everybody acknowledges it. I do nothing but drink beer and colour a pipe and sit all day long in the shade talking vacantly … I have utterly abjured all poetry, both for reading & writing. I look at the rising moon unmoved. – I wad my mental ears against all manner of sentiments. I systematically train myself into a consistent brutality. I'm utterly changed; – it is all the reaction from you.[45]

A certain degree of brutality could be seen as manly; a too great a display of tenderness dangerous in a masculine world where demonstrative affection for another male might be mistaken for sexual desire. Such a callous display of self-discipline by Beck might also have been a denial of his own homosexual feelings. Now, he offered only the cool advice of a friend: 'For yourself, I can only repeat be as jolly as you can and don't go near Cambridge till you can help it: then, after 4 months absence you will greet it with joy not ennui.'[46]

After the blow from Beck, he sought comfort from Oates, pleading with him to come down to Brighton: 'It would be very jolly if we could sit out on the beach together – I know whenever I see you at Cambridge you are swallowed up by friends and I can only give you a stray good morning and get the same in return'.[47] Oates lingered over his response and Carpenter, unable to bear any longer his desultory life in Brighton, returned to Cambridge. He was soon chiding Oates for continuing to neglect him:

> I wish you would answer my letters. What has become of you? Some people speculate that you are going to be married, but I am inclined to think this too good to be true. You must write and let me know about yourself: I do not want you to disappear into the cold outer space without leaving some sign or symbol.[48]

At the same time, he revealed that he had met another Cambridge man towards whom he was drawn:

> [He] has very quick affections and warm feelings and often times feels lonely enough up here in this somewhat chilly atmosphere and then he gets fits of extreme depression, which I am afraid is like you too, and cannot push them off for a long time and passes sleepless nights and unprofitable days.[49]

Oates was almost certainly the first person with whom Carpenter was able to talk frankly about his homosexuality. It was too bad, he told him, that they should be tormented by 'unsubstantiated devils'. Young men in love with their own sex whilst living in a cloistered world of affected manliness; fearful of their own longings and unable to connect; forced into concealment and burdened with guilt. There was a need for *comradeship*: 'I often think what fools we are not to league ourselves together by closer bonds of friendship against such evil onslaughts, for all the devils in the world would vanish – for me – if I had but one person to help me against them.'[50]

Oates responded: 'I think that I see a track opening up before me and that you have been helping me to find it. But then, oh the sickening dread that I am all too weak to undertake the fight, that I was never meant to lead, but should have been glad to follow in the tracks which others had prepared for me'.[51] He was writing from Italy, where he could be true to his sexual feelings: 'I must tell you of the charming fellow that I met in Naples … I thought myself quite blasé, yet I cannot describe to you the effect that parting from this man had upon one – the chances were so entirely against our ever meeting again'. The experience prompted some lines on the furtive encounters of those seeking what was forbidden, 'hands joined at evening but to part at dawn'.[52]

The 'long and delightful' letter from Oates made Carpenter 'restless and envious for new worlds', new freedoms, and new experiences:

> I should like to have seen your friend. There is something by itself in meeting people for a few days 'en route'. You meet openly & freely; no horrid precedents stand as a bar to intercourse, the future makes no demand of you; and so, often, you can speak of things to such a one which you can breathe to no other friend.[53]

For some, travel to the south, particularly to Italy, would come to mean freedom from inhibition; from guilt and public censure. These were places where many lovers of their own sex found both psychological and sexual liberation; lands that were hospitable to their cultural and sexual interests. They journeyed there, 'for classical ruins and Renaissance art, for sun and sea, and for the youths whom they could seduce with love or money'.[54]

On Easter Monday 1872, Maurice died. A light had gone out. Carpenter's friend Henry Salt, who believed that he had taken holy orders, 'in misunderstanding of the real purpose of his life', but having done so, could not easily detach himself: 'I remember him telling me what a struggle it cost him, respecting and loving Maurice, to give up his Orders ... He had lost all belief in the Church and its doctrines, but felt that if Maurice could acquiesce in them, it was not for him to rebel'.[55]

Before his death, Maurice had relieved him of his clerical duties but he continued with his lecturing and other College work. The year dragged on, with his daily round undertaken in a torpid, perfunctory manner. Now, academic life itself became toilsome. Frustrated by the everlasting discussion of ideas that seemed to be unrelated to actual life, by cheap philosophising and ornamental cleverness, he came to regard his donnish existence as 'a fraud and a weariness'. 'The prospect of spending the rest of my life in that atmosphere terrified me; and as I had seemed to see already the vacuity and falsity of society life at Brighton, so in another form I seemed to see the same thing [there]'.[56] In the autumn, feeling ill and incapacitated, he decided that he needed to get away from Cambridge, to regain his health and consider his future.

Apart from his mother, he named one other woman as having had a formative influence on his early life: a woman who motivated and inspired him and to whom he could turn for comfort and guidance in times of difficulty. Jane Daubeney, a worldly woman of fifty, came into his life through the marriage of one of his sisters. Their conversations on many subjects 'served to liberate my mind, corrected in many respects the native vagueness of my thought, and certainly helped me greatly on the road to choose my own way in life'.[57]

A scrap of a letter from her, written at this time of doubt, has survived:

It is terrible to me to know how you suffer. Your letter last night made me cold to the finger ends. One thing is clear … your present life is intolerable, change it you must … to think how you have suffered and how you will suffer – alas, alas! But not from any death, thank Heavens, of your powers, these I know to be great enough to float you 'high and dry' over everything. As for failure dear, you will not fail though in truth you will have plenty of hard work but whatever the world may say failure is not scandalous [a reference to the break-up of her own marriage]. When you get away from the depressing influence of your present life, with all its worries, you will breathe and clap your hands and thank God! The term is over I see on the 16th … Then dear sweet thing you will come out of this.[58]

Recollecting her own happy times growing up in Italy, she urged him to take a long holiday there. By now, he did not need much persuading. Pleading poor health, he was granted a long leave of absence, a boundless time before he would have to return to Cambridge; time enough, he told Oates, for 'the birth of a living soul'.[59]

He left for Rome in the middle of January. Having known little except the closed societies of Brighton and Cambridge, it was liberating. Under the healing influences of air and sun, all the questions that had been tormenting him faded away: 'I thought about them no more; but new elements came into my life which decided them for me'.[60] Wandering amidst the rich records of antiquity, sculpture had a deep effect upon him. Pictures were interesting, but the statuary 'had something more, a germinative influence on my mind, which adding itself to and corroborating the effect of Whitman's poetry, left with me, as it were, the seed of new conceptions of life'.[61] To come to such an awareness amidst the delicate air and delightful landscape of Italy marked both an end and a beginning.

After Rome he moved on to the Bay of Naples and Capri, 'beautiful and picturesque beyond expression'. Early April found him back in Rome for a further month of languid idleness, before travelling on to Florence, his final destination, where he stayed long enough to see the fireflies skim and flicker over the blossoming wheat fields. By the time he returned home, such a change of outlook had taken place that a return to his Cambridge life was now impossible. He wrote to Oates: 'I have just this instant arrived [back] and in a moment I shall have to go and see the Master about my relinquishing Orders. He is in a dreadful way'.[62]

He may have tired of academic life, but scattered among the notes prepared for the sermons delivered during 1870 and 1871 are very clear indications of the real root of his estrangement. It was the burden of his sexuality; the strain of concealing his feelings for men. Untruthfulness was 'a work of degradation and darkness'. In the 'obscurity of deceit' an individual was 'lonely and exposed to every danger.'[63] Although he would put a loss of faith about as the reason for resigning his fellowship, it was not 'the final and convincing thing' but a smokescreen. It was the Church's disavowal of human sexuality and, especially, its abhorrence of love between men that drove him out. As he would later write, under its strictures, thousands 'allowed their lives to be maimed and blighted, their health and personal well-being ruined'.[64] In *Towards Democracy*, he will give voice to his then terror:

> Was it really your own anxious face you used to keep catching
> in the glass? … did you once desire to shine among your peers
> – or did you shrink from the knowledge of your own defects
> in the midst of them? … Are you tormented with inordinate
> clutching lusts of which you dare not speak? Are you nearly
> mad with the sting of them, and nearly mad with the terror lest
> they should betray you?[65]

Faced with the prospect that his whole Cambridge career was likely to come to an end, he entertained the idea of taking up writing as a profession. When he broached the idea with his more honest friends, they were quick to reinforce his doubts: 'I well remember the derisive chorus of the other Fellows which greeted (at some College meeting or other) the announcement of my intention!'[66] Although cautioned by these well-meant responses, he decided to stay in Brighton during the summer and work on producing a slim volume of verse. He found it difficult to write anything new; gathered together some existing verses and sought a publisher. 'Of course, no publisher would take the volume at his risk, and I was content, after a few efforts, to pay the piper myself for the pleasure of seeing the work in print, and on the chance of its leaping to a world-wide success!'[67]

In November he was in Cannes when he received reviews of this first literary venture.[68] A writer in the *Athenaeum* described the collection as 'Keats writ indeed in water'. He was aware that the poems were mere contrivances, attempts to emulate a certain literary style and standard. The real significance of the volume was its very discreet, coded homoeroticism. Although he would say that there was 'not much of the author's own self in it', some poems pointed to intense sexual and religious preoccupations. Putting the reviews aside, as he often did when life seemed to be against him, he looked to Whitman for consolation. 'I have returned to Walt W ... He is very refreshing. I like some of the *Songs of the World* very much,' he told Charles Oates.[69] The opening verse of *Song of the Open Road* gave the impetus for what was to be the most important decision of his life: 'Afoot and light-hearted I take to the open road/Healthy, free, the world before me/The long brown path before me leading wherever I choose'.[70] On the journey back to Cambridge the question of what he might do was constantly revolving in his mind. How would he support himself? With his fellowship and lectureship his income was considerable for the time and prospects were good for the future. If he abandoned his orders, he would probably lose his fellowship and possibly have to leave Cambridge altogether. Was it reasonable, he asked himself, to risk all this, for what might after all be only a 'Quixotic fancy'? Then, 'it suddenly flashed upon me, with a vibration through my whole body, that I would and must somehow go and make my life with the mass of the people and the manual workers'.[71] He had absorbed Whitman's call to:

despise riches, give alms to everyone that asks, stand up for the stupid and crazy, devote your income and labour to others, hate tyrants, argue not concerning God, have patience and indulgence towards the people, take off your hat to nothing known or unknown or to any man or number of men, go freely with powerful uneducated persons and with the young …[72]

Whitman had worked his spell, as he had with others, 'saved them from their own little selves – from their own little virtues and vices – and united them in the solidarity of humanity'.[73]

When family, friends, fellows of the College and others urged him not to take such a step he felt a strong obligation to go through the formality of seeking a lay fellowship, but it was decided that if he renounced his orders he could not possibly remain at the College, 'owing to the scandal of the thing'. So, he engaged a solicitor to set in train the process of ecclesiastical law that would enable him to renounce his orders. He was fortunate: before the passing of the Clerical Disabilities Relief Act in 1870, he would have been bound irrevocably to his calling and required to remain the Reverend Edward Carpenter for the rest of his life. In June 1874, he surrendered all the rights and privileges belonging to the office of priest.

With his departure from Cambridge imminent, he wrote his first letter to Whitman. 'I couldn't help it', 'I wanted to tell him how things are going on in England and that he has readers'[74] It was an intensely personal letter: '[T]here are many things which I find it hard to say to anyone here. And for my sake you must not mind reading what I have written.'[75] He wanted to speak for those in England for whom reading Whitman had been the dawning of a new day, and become 'the central point of their lives'; an allusion to the effect of his homoerotic poetry on many individuals who Carpenter would come to know.

Of democracy, he told Whitman that in England, 'I think I see the new, open, life which is to come; the spirit moving backwards and forwards beneath the old forms … but the flower is very far and we do not dare to think even what it will be like'. But there was hope in the struggles of women and in the growing self-consciousness of the working class.[76]

Only after sharing his political affinities with Whitman did he turn to what he really wanted to say, and which he hoped Whitman would 'not mind' reading. The previous day a young workman had come to mend his door, 'with the old divine light in his eyes'. Was he recalling the line in Whitman's poem 'Among the Multitude': 'I perceive one picking me out by secret and divine signs'. It is difficult to read it otherwise, for it was this incident with the workman 'more than anything' that had made him write to Walt: 'Because you have, as it were, given me a ground for the love of men I thank you continually in my heart. (And others thank you though they do not say so). For you have made men to be not ashamed of the noblest instinct of their nature. Women are beautiful; but to some, there is that which passes the love of women'.[77] Although love for the male had to be elevated, ennobled and idealised, what was *instinctual* was being sexually attracted to other men. However much such love was 'spiritualised', and had to be in a homophobic society, it was Whitman's 'treatment of sex' that had produced the 'great leap of joy' when Carpenter first discovered his poetry.[78]

Finally, he turned to his future, to the new life to which Whitman had pointed the way:

I was in orders; but I have given that up – utterly. It was no good. Nor does the University do: there is nothing vital in it. Now I am going away to lecture to working men and women in the North. They at least desire to lay hold of something with a real grasp. And I can give something of mathematics and science. It may be of no use, but I shall see.[79]

When it seemed that he would not be offered a lay fellowship, he explored the possibility of joining the university's extension programme, which had been inaugurated that year, and was offered a post. Its aims were explicitly egalitarian: to open up university education and to free it from class privilege. Its objectives chimed with his socialistic outlook and the siren call of Whitmanic democracy. Whitman despised the 'great pumpkins' of Harvard and rejoiced to learn that Carpenter had escaped from such a world with his humanity intact; had 'plucked himself from the burning'. He would say of this letter: 'It is beautiful, like a confession … I seem to get very near to his heart and he to mine in that letter: it has a place in our personal history – an important place.'[80]

3

A New Life

He had never been to the northern towns; was completely ignorant of industrial England, of the inhabitants of these grimy soot-laden places, of their manners and customs. His tenuous acquaintance with 'the mass people' had been with diminutive servants at home and college bed-makers. He knew nothing of the diverse trades found in these distant places, and was only vaguely aware of the fervour of their dissenting sects and political agitations. In Brighton, a while before embarking upon what was to be a life-changing journey, he penned some lines of nostalgia, and hope:

These are the days which nourished and fed me so kindly and well; this is the place where I was born, the walls and roofs which are familiar to me, the windows out of which I have looked … This is the overshadowing love and care of parents; these are the faces and deeds, indelible, of brothers and sisters – closing round me like a wall – the early world in which I lay so long … This is today: the little ship lies ready, the fresh air blowing, the sunlight pouring over the world. These are the gates of all cities and habitations standing open ...[1]

When he arrived in Leeds in October 1874, he imagined that he would be absorbed at once into the daily routines and pulse of life of real humanity. He had finally made his escape from the coteries of elegant and learned people at Cambridge. But what was wished for was not to be immediately given. From the first day, his life was ordered by the 'advanced' women who held sway in the organisation of the university extension movement. But the arrival of this handsome well-connected eligible bachelor produced a frisson of excitement and he was soon drawn into their intrigues; with pressing invitations to meet for *tete-a-tete* afternoon tea in the gas-reeking rooms of their villa residences. Such encounters, no doubt to the disappointment of his hosts, did not lead to headlong adoration or offers of marriage. If they could never give him what he desired, such women, with strong decisive minds, would always be attractive to him. The local organising secretary was uncompromising in her demands for her sex and habitually peppered her conversations with thrusts at the male population. After his credentials had been probed, he was invited to feminist meetings, which gave him his first contact with the fledgling women's movement. The empathy that he already felt for women prepared to fight against their subordination would, in time, enable him to forge enduring alliances.

His students were certainly a disappointment. Instead of the horny-handed artisans that he had envisaged they were mainly 'young lady types'; girls like his own sisters, living at home and having nothing in particular to do, together with older spinsterish women suffering the same plight. Of the remainder, there were a few elderly clerks, one or two 'extra-intelligent' young men, and, lastly, a very small sprinkling of manual workers.

He began his new life by giving a course of lectures on astronomy, a curious subject to be teaching in smoke-hidden towns where a star could seldom be seen. If he dragged a class onto the local moor, invariably the subjects of discussion would withdraw from observation. At Cambridge, his sermons had been chiselled twenty-minute homilies, carefully written out and delivered in an atmosphere of disinterestedness. Now, he had to talk for an hour; to engage an attentive audience hanging upon his every word, scribbling down his utterances, and eager to engage him in conversation afterwards. It was a total contrast to Cambridge, where he had found students' dullness and distaste for their work crushing.

He was also lecturing at Halifax and Skipton and the sheer physical effort of travelling from one town to another, plagued by persistent bouts of exhaustion and nervous tension, was draining. He would arrive in a town an hour or two before his meeting, dragging a heavy box of apparatus. Then, he would have to set up experiments, usually in some bleak schoolroom. He often got home 'a vibrating mass of nerves', only to rise the next day to face going through a similar round.

After eighteen months of such toil, seeking respite he made a journey that had the characteristics of a pilgrimage. He went to America to meet Whitman. 'By day and night, the presence of this Friend, exhaled from his own books, had been with me – thus working, transforming, and drawing me wonderfully to seek him'.[2] The exchange of letters had drawn them closer, and after Whitman sent him a gift of a complete edition of his poetry his desire to meet him became overpowering. In late April 1877, he fulfilled his 'long-slumbering intention'. Drawing on friends, he got introductions to Emerson and Wendell Holmes.

When meeting Emerson, he mentioned that he was going to see Whitman, at which he made an odd whinnying sound and exclaimed: 'Well, I thought he had some merit at one time: there was a good deal of promise in the first edition [*Leaves of Grass*] – Burt he is a wayward fanciful man'.[3] It was Emerson's salutation, 'I greet you at the beginning of a great career' that Whitman, without his permission, had attached to the second edition of *Leaves of Grass*. He found Wendell Holmes to be a 'good-natured little spiteful creature' who had little better to say of Whitman. 'The poets *coquette* with Nature and weave garlands of roses for her; but Whitman *goes at her* like a great hirsuit man – no it won't do'. He revealed that, when he was in the company of Lowell and Longfellow, Longfellow had commented: 'Walt might have done something if he had only had a decent training and education.'[4]

With such 'commendations' still ringing in his ears, he knocked at the door of 43 Stevens Street, Camden, where Walt was living with his brother Colonel George Whitman and his wife. He waited a few minutes in the sitting-room while Walt was called. He came down the stairs slowly, leaning heavily on the banisters and dragging his partially paralysed leg, the result of a stroke in 1873. At first sight, he appeared quite old, with a long grey, almost white, beard and shaggy head and neck. But he was tall and erect, and at closer sight not so old; with a florid fresh complexion, pure grey-blue eyes and strong, well-formed hands:

> I was most struck, in his face, by the high arch of his eyebrows, giving a touch of child-like wonder and contemplation to his expression; yet his eyes, though full of a kind of wistful tenderness were essentially not contemplative but perceptive – active rather than receptive – lying far back, steady, clear, with small definite pupils and heavy lids of passion and experience.[5]

At the foot of the stairs, he took Edward's hand and said, 'I was afraid we should miss after all' – referring to a previous call he had made when Walt was not at home. Having found him a seat, and only then leaving hold of his hand, he sat down himself and conversation soon turned to England and his friends there. Edward had found Emerson and Wendell Holmes self-absorbed; interested in little but literary matters; seemingly caring little for America's progress or its place in the world. He soon found that

Walt 'in interest and grandeur of personality out-towered them'. The turbulent Niagara Falls was the only thing that he saw during his visit that seemed quite to match him in spirit. In their first ten minutes together, he wrote later, he became conscious of an 'immense vista or background in his personality'. He had been unclear in his mind about Walt's character, thinking that he was perhaps eccentric, unbalanced, even violent, but this meeting produced quite a contrary effect. Whitman was considerate, courteous, 'with a simplicity of manner and freedom from 'egotistic wrigglings'.[6]

After further talk, Whitman suggested that they should take a trip across to Philadelphia. Putting on his grey slouch hat (an attire that Edward, in conscious imitation or otherwise, would also sport), he sallied forth with evident pleasure. Taking Edward's arm for support, they walked slowly the best part of a mile to the ferry. The life of the streets and its people were near and dear to Whitman. The men on the ferries were old friends, some old lovers, and when they landed on the Philadelphia side they were 'quite besieged'. They rambled through Philadelphia, mainly using the tramcars, a venue for numerous amorous encounters by Whitman. When they reached the ferry to return the last bell was ringing. They might have caught it but Whitman was not in a hurry. The boat went and they sat down, laughing and talking until another arrived.

A few days later, Walt went into the country to stay at the farm of his 'dear and valued friends' the Staffords, and Edward was invited to visit them. Walt had met one of their sons, Harry, in a printer's office in Camden and they soon became lovers. He would often stay at the farm for weeks or months at a time and his chief delight was to spend part of his day by a little lake a short distance from the house, where he would sit for hours enjoying the sight of frolicking naked youths.

In gay circles, there is a long-standing story that a sexual encounter with Whitman took place during this visit. But the idea that there was any such intimacy other than affection; a friendly kiss, is fanciful. Whitman, like Wilde, was only sexually attracted to young men. When Wilde visited Whitman, in January 1882, it is suggested that they 'talked of nothing but pretty boys'.[7] Carpenter's ideal sexual partner was a strong, mature, slightly younger man, or a man of his own age. He was then aged thirty-three and Whitman, now partially disabled, was fifty-eight. Charley Shively, in his account of Whitman's boy-lovers,[8] wrote that Edward took up right away with Whitman's Timber Creek boys. Harry Stafford was nineteen at the time and it is not improbable that there was some philandering with the sexually-frustrated Carpenter. He asked after Harry in subsequent letters to Whitman, who sent him a photograph of the young man. There may, also, have been dalliances with other youths, whose native openness of character and directness Carpenter would have found novel and inviting. In later life, young men would figure prominently in his romantic dalliances.

Walt's evident contentment and inner-peace brought home to him the emotional emptiness in his own life. He had met two of America's literary luminaries, travelled through magnificent countryside, experienced the novelty and quaintness of the ways of life of both prosperous and poor Americans, yet the inner void remained: 'I was alone all this time, and felt lonely, but as it was the same in England there was nothing remarkable about it'.[9]

On his return home, forced to resume his humdrum life, he swore a great oath that somehow, he would break free. Attracted by the heartiness of its folk, he decided to settle in Sheffield, and through his lectures began to build up alliances. 'I felt I had come into, or at least in sight of, the world to which I belonged, and to my natural *habitat*'.[10] One evening after a lecture, a man of about his own age struck up a conversation. He was Albert Fearnehough, a scythe-maker who lived with his wife and two children in a cottage on the farm of his friend Charles Fox (who was also at the lecture). 'In many ways he was delightful to me, as the one powerful uneducated and natural person I had as yet in all my life met with'.[11] Fearnehough invited him to visit them in the little hamlet of Bradway, some four or more miles from Sheffield. He soon took up their invitation, and on many weekends walked out to have tea, or to just roam about the fields together. Soon he was helping with the farm work.

His friendship with the two men was a catalyst: 'I saw at last my way of escape out of that dingy wilderness, that *selva obscura*, in which I had wandered lost, from childhood even down to the very middle of life's journey'.[12] He was soon seized by the idea of an invigorating outdoor life. The open air, the hardiness of sun and wind, would build up his strength and combat his recurring bouts of ill health. He formed a plan, 'of coming to live if possible, with these good people, and carrying on my lectures even from this distance out in the country'.[13] When approached, Fearnehough, finding Carpenter as much a new dimension in his life as he was in Carpenter's, invited him to lodge with the family and in May 1880 he 'migrated' there. For the first time, he lived cheek by jowl with a working-class man and his family.

The death of his mother in 1881, and a little more than a year later of his father, broke the bond of filial loyalty. All the pent-up feelings of despair and hopelessness secretly expressed in scraps of disconnected prose and poetry burst forth like a broken damn. That year, Arunachalam had sent him a copy of the *Bhagavad Gita*. It opened his eyes to the sacred, religious-infused, literature of the vast Indian continent, and 'curiously liberated and set in movement the mass of material which had already formed within me and which was then waiting to take shape … It gave me the needed cue, and concatenated my work to the Eastern tradition.'[14] The result of this special state of mind was to be the most creative, if for some unfathomable, of all his work. As he wrote, it was the outcome of 'a kind of super consciousness' that lay beyond the purely intellectual. It, 'came first, as a Vision, so to speak, and a revelation – as a great body of feeling and intuition which I had to put into words as best I could'.[15] It seemed already there: 'I never hesitated for a moment. Day by day it came along from point to point. I did not hurry; I expressed everything with slow care and to my best; I utilized former material which I had by me; but the one illuminating mood remained and everything fell into place under it'.[16] He became totally absorbed, and the need for time to write grew so strong, that he realised that to continue with his lecturing round would sap this creative energy. He threw it up and felt supremely happy.

Early in 1883, the outcome of his intense labour, *Towards Democracy*, the work that was to immediately define him, was published. It was a powerful, critique of the very foundations of late-Victorian society, and an unburdening of years of repressed feelings about his sexuality and his social entrapment; a frank self-disclosure, a confession, healthy and joyous. It was his 'coming out'. He was eager to tell Walt:

> It is in paragraphs, some short (half a line or so), some long, in the ordinary prose form, tho' poetical in character. It is a good deal made up of previous writings of the last five or six years squeezed out – a drop or two here or there. I have thought for some time of calling it Towards Democracy and I do not see any reason for altering the title – though the word Democracy does not often occur in it.[17]

But *democracy* is one of its central ideas. It has a peculiar, even esoteric, usage. He does not mean a definite form of political organisation or government. It is both prior to and beyond organisation. Democracy is conceived in the sense of a Platonic *idea* and the word is used chiefly in a mystical, idealistic, sense. It means the conscious realisation of the union of all life and the expression of the universal self through the individual. Understood as such, it denotes a vast affiliation of selves, a Celestial City of equals.

If, as a work, it was irregular in form and uneven in quality, three clear interconnected themes ran through the work: the *personal*, concerned with his own self-deliverance; the *transcendental*, centred on the imperative of a unification of man with nature; and the *social*, a condemnation of the 'civilisation' that represented the loss of this unity.

Its intellectual coherence was of secondary importance. It had been written, as he said, in a mood of illumination and inspiration under the pressure of feeling. Whatever its defects, the uniqueness of its conception convinced him never to make alterations to the original text. He would always consider this first part of *Towards Democracy*, which really stands apart from its succeeding three parts (to be published over the next twenty years), to be the spiritual centre from which his later books would radiate. It was a veritable storehouse.

Five-hundred copies were printed at his expense. For whatever reason, the volume did not carry his name, and only the words 'Bradway 1881–82', placed at the very end of the volume, gave any clue to the author's identity. The infant, if it did not exactly fall still-born from the press, in his own words, 'showed hardly any signs of life'. The literary establishment either ignored it or jeered at it as the ravings of some anonymous author. Perhaps, if he had been writing from the security of his Cambridge college, his offerings might have reached 'polite society', but how could the world be expected to listen to the companion of farm and factory hands? The then Master, of his old college, Sir Henry Maine, would include passages from it in his *Popular Government*, as the strongest evidence of an over-excited state of mind. Many years later, Carpenter humorously summarised its prospects:

> That it should go its own way quietly, neither applauded by the crowd, nor barked at by the dogs, but knocking softly here and there at a door and finding friendly hospitality is surely its most gracious and satisfying destiny.[18]

A collection of poems in Whitmanesque form was unlikely to please those schooled in iambic verse. It was Whitman's disregard for conventional literary forms, as much as his dubious morality, which had antagonised some English critics. Inevitably, the comparisons with Whitman were seized upon and the always slightly opprobrious title of the 'English Whitman' became firmly attached to him.

Those who saw *Towards Democracy* as a pale imitation of Whitman's *Leaves of Grass* did not look beyond its free-verse style, such was the novelty in England of this form of prosody. The real connections were much deeper than the superficial similarity of prose style and, importantly, were not so much logical as psychological. In each, from the very first line, intellectual clarity was subordinated to emotional expression. Each work was a rhapsodic self-revelation and a universalising of their own natures: every individual life contained the elements of all humanity. He also shared with Whitman his critique of contemporary sexual ideology and the aspiration to write male homoerotic desire into a new sexual and social synthesis. Both wished to enfranchise the sexual body, not simply to defend man-to-man love.

Whereas Carpenter soon made his own sexual 'self' explicit, certainly by the second (1885) edition of *Towards Democracy*, Whitman was a life-long reviser of the 'self', as he was a persistent reviser of the text. In a puritan world, where *Leaves of Grass* was placed in a locked case at Harvard, lest it threatened students' morals, his emotional honesty was compromised. There is little doubt that the chants 'Song of Myself' and 'I Sing the Body Electric' were calls for sexual liberation, but the truth of his homosexuality and the homosexual themes of *Leaves of Grass* were both cloaked in a self-confessed deviousness. He would tell Carpenter that there were truths that it was 'necessary to envelop or wrap up', likening himself to a furtive hen secreting away her eggs. When finally exasperated by John Addington Symonds's persistence in asking him whether 'adhesiveness' condoned the physical expression of male comradeship, Whitman responded by claiming paternity of six children! His calculated ambiguities ensured that his 'life below the life' remained concealed, and his role in the struggle for homosexual liberation in America during his own lifetime negligible. His denials contrasted sharply with Carpenter's 'trumpet blasts for the invert's recognition even in the very first version of *Towards Democracy*'.[19] From his first reading of Whitman's poems he was sure that, for all his artifice, whether through sensible caution or cowardice, he was addressing him and his kind. Whitman had provided 'a thrilling invitation to self-recognition, fraternity and empowerment'.[20]

Having found his literary voice, he might have settled into an armchair-life of scholarly endeavour congenial to many Victorian gentlemen, but no sooner had his father died than he made up his mind to acquire a piece of land outside Sheffield. He had been seized by the invigorating outdoor life and the pleasure of manual labour. Now nothing but such an existence would satisfy him. With some legacies, his share of his father's estate and his savings, he had quite a large fortune. He told Charles Oates:

> I am looking out for a small homestead with about ten acres of land near Sheffield, freehold, where I can embark on some agricultural work – chiefly fruit-growing – with the assistance of two friends who have some experience in that line. I do not wish to leave Sheffield as I have such a number of good friends here – of all classes but chiefly 'the people'.[21]

For many months he scoured the countryside around Sheffield looking for what lay in his mind's eye. Eventually, he found a small-holding in the little hamlet of Millthorpe, a dozen dwellings nestling in the Cordwell Valley in the parish of Holmesfield, between Sheffield and Chesterfield. It was a delightful setting, but he thought it too far from Sheffield for him to keep up any sort of life there. Although he had told Oates of his desire to stay in the district, he began to look further afield, travelling down country as far as Worcestershire. It was fortuitous for his life to come that he failed to find anything which suited him so far south. He returned to Millthorpe.

As well as its distance from Sheffield, the plot of land had seemed too small, even for the modest project that he had in mind. There were only three smallish fields, amounting to about seven acres, but the land was good and the spot had a sylvan beauty. Along the bottom perimeter of the plot a little brook, barely more than a yard wide, scampered down through the fields from the moorland a mile away, feeding the wheel of an adjacent corn-mill, which had given its name to the hamlet. Beyond rose the gentle slopes of a sparsely wooded hill with browsing cattle and a township of rabbits. Over the brow lay a beautiful wooded valley and a mile or so away stretched the open moor.

He could hardly have found a more old-world, purely agricultural parish than Holmesfield. It survived in the old rural style: the long day with its varied tasks, the cattle and the crops, the barn and the public-house. He was still apprehensive about living so far from Sheffield, 'completely gulfed in the country', but buried his lingering doubts and bought the land the following Easter. In a flurry of activity, he engaged a builder and had a two-storeyed stone cottage erected. In October 1883, with Albert Fearnehough and his family, he stepped over the threshold into his little kingdom. With Fearnehough and some hired labour, he worked for whole days out in his fields or in the garden, digging drains, going into Chesterfield for supplies, loading and fetching manure, going to the coal-pit, grooming and bedding down the horse that had been acquired; getting off to market at 6 a.m. with vegetables and fruit piled on a cart with 'Edward Carpenter, Market Gardener, Millthorpe' painted on its side, then standing behind a stall until the early afternoon. Although, from time to time, his health suffered under the unaccustomed labour, it improved markedly during the next few years and he became physically stronger than at any time in his life. More significantly, his 'nerve troubles' connected with his previous mode of life were thrown off completely. But he always longed for more sunshine and the company of more vivacious people. Nude bathing in the stream that flowed at the bottom of the garden was more than bracing in the northern climes and every two or three years he would go off with one or more friends to Italy, the South of France or the islands of Corsica and Sicily. He loved the shores of the Mediterranean.

Life at Millthorpe was congenial to his work and tastes: in close contact with nature, moving freely among undemanding country folk and combining outdoor manual labour with his literary work. He was to be on easy terms with farmers and their hands, although it was clear from their respectful manner towards him that they were conscious of his different social status. He would come to admire their serenity, good humour and tenacity. Even their irritating silent ways were a relief from 'the eternal gabble of the cities'. But he did not expect them to bring about their own emancipation. He found an absolute acceptance of things as they were; a complete non-interest in reform, and a positive indifference to anything not patently visible to the eye. The urban working-class was another matter. There, he found empathy, so much so that he boasted that if he were put down suddenly in one of the large northern manufacturing towns he would be in friendly touch with some artisans before the day was out. Within its midst, he saw the ferment of the new life coming on; the dream of a better future and the efforts to realise it; the greater alertness and thirst for education, and the busy hum and activity of the new trades unions and labour associations. It was good to have roots in the countryside, but it was necessary to have branches in the great towns, where alone it was possible to come into contact with the winds and storms of human life. The town, even with its often physical wretchedness, was the centre of all progressive thinking. Millthorpe was never an escape from this seething humanity.

He was soon writing to Walt to tell him about his new life:

> Just a line to give you my changed address. I have been here since October last – very busy all last summer getting a little homestead built, and this winter digging and planting – have about seven acres altogether – we are gardening about two acres; fruit, flowers and vegetables; have about two and a half acres grass and about the same quantity part wheat for ourselves and part oats for the horse. My friends the Fearnehoughs have come with me, and we are employing one or two extra hands besides, just now. It is a beautiful valley right up against the Derbyshire moors, but warm; we are about eight miles from Sheffield and five and a half from Chesterfield – three and a half from the nearest station. There is a quite old flour mill here, from which the place no doubt takes its name; very quaint old wooden wheels and cogs – the stream which feeds it runs at the bottom of my three fields – lots of wood and water all about the valley.[22]

He had made his home in the countryside at a time of growing antipathy to urban life, to cities and grimy manufacturing towns peopled by what were seen by many as dehumanised wage-slaves living with poverty and disease. There was a deep questioning, particularly by middle-class intellectuals, of the moral superiority of the new industrial order. For a good many, abhorrence and nostalgia combined to produce a desire for a pastoral existence. But such a yearning was, paradoxically, against the background of an economic decline of large parts of the countryside under the progressive encroachment of urban settlements, which had denuded many villages of their populations. The desire for a more natural life also attracted those for whom Victorian conventions and proprieties prevented the expression of spontaneous feeling.

A simpler form of living based on more natural relationships was seen to be more possible in rural settings. There was no coherent movement: attempts to establish self-sufficient agricultural communities and to revive handicrafts coalesced with other anti-urban, anti-commercial impulses. There was a rejection of restrictive bourgeois behavioural codes and conventions, and a new aesthetic of simple, plain furniture in place of the ornate. The appeal of spiritualism, transcendental and pantheistic religions, as alternatives to a beleaguered Christianity also gave the natural world a deeper meaning for many.

If later credited with it, Carpenter never intended that Millthorpe should be an experiment in co-operative farming or communal living. This is one of a number of claims that, through constant repetition, have crept into the Carpenter 'legend'. There *was* no such agenda; no idea of this kind in his mind at the time. He felt the need for his new way of life directly and instinctively, not as something argued out and intellectually concluded. It was a life shorn of bourgeois conventions, from the 'circle of endlessly complaisant faces bowing you back from reality'.[23] Despite occasional misgivings, he counted his blessings. He had satisfied his 'root-demands'. He was buried in a beautiful Derbyshire valley. There was no resident squire and the church, together with its incumbent, was 'quite amiably remote'. He contrasted this with life in Brighton and Cambridge. No more of that. In a symbolic act he gave away his dress clothes. William Morris, on the day he resigned his directorship of Devon Great Consuls, a joint-stock company founded by his family, deliberately sat down on his top hat.

As Henry Salt shrewdly observed, temperamentally Carpenter was the last person who could have devoted himself permanently to agricultural work of any kind. He was once at Millthorpe during hay-cutting time and along with some other guests volunteered to help with the work. The novelty of manual labour sustained the townies through the morning and after a leisurely mid-day meal they all felt obliged to show a mock enthusiasm by returning to their toil:

> I thought our host did not look quite so pleased with us as we were entitled to expect, but out we all went in the blazing afternoon sun ... Suddenly Edward, who was next in the line to me, threw down his hay-fork and said testily: 'Well, I can't go on all day cocking this stuff, if *you* can.' So, virtue was rewarded and all the weary had rest.[24]

As Salt's presence testified, Millthorpe became an escape for Carpenter's cosmopolitan friends from the south. In time, it would serve as a place of *rendezvous* 'for all classes and conditions of society'; offering fellowship for 'progressives' and 'unrespectables' alike; for all individuals, high and low, who felt alienated by the spiritual bankruptcy of commercialism and the horrors of industrial capitalism. Its ethos was not so much utopian as egalitarian. Over the years, he would boast, railway clerks, engine-drivers, signalmen, naval and military officers, Cambridge and Oxford dons, students and advanced women all made their way there. He pictured it as a melting pot of the classes: 'Young colliers from the neighbouring mines put on the boxing-gloves with sprigs of aristocracy; learned professors sat down to table with farm-lads'.[25] His prolonged, deep-seated hostility towards the class from which he had sprung did not lead to estrangement from his family, for sisters and brothers visited and stayed in nearby cottages.

To his chagrin, as his writing on many topical subjects struck a vein, faddists of all kinds – vegetarians, dress reformers, temperance workers, spiritualists, secularists, anti-vivisectionists – sought him out. Then there were the individuals whose knowledge of nature was limited to idyllic literature and weekends in the country. The expert builders of social systems also came to his door, finding, perhaps to their surprise, a man who distrusted, even detested, rigid systems and hard moral rules, refusing to bind himself to any that were not founded on the universality of human nature and human needs. But his openness to ideas and people, 'the man that will wear sandals and invites anybody into his garden',[26] made him an easy target for many single-minded campaigners. He was sympathetic to many of these causes, and indulged himself in some; each in its way a small prick against bourgeois life. Although he wrote articles and made speeches on many of these topics, they always remained peripheral to his central life-interests.

4

Eros the Great Leveller

Carpenter would muse, 'how often Uranians of good position and breeding are drawn to rougher types, as of manual workers, and frequently very permanent alliances grow up in this way ...'[1] In the brief history of his sexual life written for Havelock Ellis, he declared:

> [M]y ideal of love is a powerful strongly built man of my own age or rather younger – preferably of the working class. Though having solid sense and character he need not be especially intellectual. If endowed in the latter way, he must not be too glib or refined. Anything effeminate in a man, or anything of the cheap intellectual style, repels me very decisively.[2]

Many lovers of their own sex were drawn to the working-classes. Edward Fitzgerald, translator of *The Rubáiyát of Omar Khayam*, was famously enamoured of a young, illiterate fisherman. After reading Carlyle's *Heroes*, Fitzgerald acquainted his friend with his own hero, 'neither Prince, Poet, nor Man of Letters, but Captain of a Lowestoft Lugger'.[3] Carpenter's friend Charles Ashbee, a pioneer of the Arts and Crafts movement, was happiest in the company of young London East End working-class men, who best met his idealised vision of male comradeship. Another friend, Goldsworthy Lowes Dickinson, confessed that his secret desire was to be trampled upon by the shiny boots of a strapping young working-class man.[4] The poet A. E. Housman was believed to have had 'a gondolier in Venice and rough trade in Paris'.[5] And another of Carpenter's friends, Edward Morgan Forster, found transient contentment with an Egyptian tram conductor and later an English policeman. Joe Ackerley, Forster's young friend, had his first glimpse of working-class masculinity in the form of a handsome boy delivering groceries to his parents' house. He afterwards found his ideal friend in a former seaman whose 'silken-skinned, muscular, perfect body was a delight to behold, like the Ephebe of Kritos. His brown-eyed, slightly simian face, with its flattened nose and full thick lips, attracted me at once'. For Ackerley and others, such friendships 'opened up interesting areas of life, hitherto unknown.'[6]

Bourgeois strictures against homosexuality made the pursuit of sexual pleasure with social equals dangerous, creating a demand for homosexual services long met by working-class individuals through a subculture of clubs, brothels, male street-walkers and compliant guardsmen. The homosexual male crossed the class divide for sex in much the same way as his heterosexual counterpart, but always with the threat of social ostracism. Trampling on class mores was subversive of social hierarchy and for some a greater offence than homosexual indecencies. But for many of his social superiors, the working-class male was the ideal erotic conquest. It was imagined that he would be more spontaneous and natural in his love-making, have fewer moral scruples and be less impeded by social conventions. And his perceived superior masculinity, his muscularity and strength, were decisive. Here was a *real* man, and doubly so if, as was often the case with soldiers, he was heterosexual. The term 'rough trade' excited the imagination, conjuring up a picture of a powerful physical type bursting with primitive sexual energy.

For John Addington Symonds, whether on the streets of London, on the canals of Venice or in the mountains of Switzerland, handsome, unsophisticated, sexually pliant young men could always be found. Angelo Fusato, his 'magnificent gondolier', was more than willing, for an appropriate number of lire, to satisfy the needs of an eccentric English gentleman. Secure in his heterosexuality, Angelo could surrender his body with grace and cheerfulness. When Symonds entered a male brothel for the first time to pass an afternoon with a brawny young soldier, the experience of sharing a bed with someone so different from himself had a powerful effect; the strapping young soldier with his frank eyes and pleasant smile, and Symonds, the 'victim of sophisticated passion':

> I learned from it – or I deluded myself into thinking I had learned – that the physical appetite of one male for another may be made the foundation of a solid friendship. Within the sphere of the male brothel, at least, permanent human relations, affections, reciprocal toleration, decencies of conduct, asking and yielding, concession and abstention, could find their natural sphere: perhaps more than in the sexual relations consecrated by middle-class matrimony.[7]

So, the comradely attitude of the soldier prepared to sell his body to a stranger seemed to suggest, but Symonds was well aware that their coming together was a form of business. At the end of the transaction, which had not involved sexual intercourse but simply his enjoyment of the close vicinity of a splendid naked piece of manhood, the conviction that 'some at least of the deepest moral problems might be solved by fraternity' remained.[8]

Being in the presence of a magnificent physical specimen gave Symonds an immense sexual thrill. There was no need for talk, even if there had been any ground for the kind of discourse that a man of sophisticated culture might have wished for. Without a need to understand the inner lives of such individuals, demanding only unsophisticated masculinity, some devalued them as persons; 'all body and no soul' as Oscar Wilde was purported to have remarked. The truth is that many used such youths and men crudely for their sexual satisfaction. Wilde, especially, took cynical advantage of the poverty of youths who prostituted themselves almost entirely for monetary and other rewards.

From the age of forty onwards, Symonds' poor health had forced him to live abroad, which distorted his thinking about the social levelling possibilities of homosexual love. Within the Swiss canton of Graubünden, where he resided, there was an absence of class distinctions and caste privileges, which made possible associations that would not have been socially sanctioned in England. It opened up opportunities for friendships and sexual encounters with 'peasants of every description, postilions, drivers, and carters, conductors of the *diligence*, carpenters' and others.[9]

Whatever he may have visualised, he inhabited social worlds that could never be reconciled. He conceitedly told a friend: 'My life is being spent too much among the great of this world. The Empress Frederick is here with her daughter Margaret and the nice young Prince of Hesse … They make considerable demands on my society. It is good for a man to live in both worlds'. The other world was, 'a little old-fashioned wine-shop in a garden of vines, where the gondoliers congregate', and where he first set eyes on Angelo Fusato.[10]

As he sat among the gondoliers, it was only his capacity to speak Italian that gave him the slightest affinity with them. His sexual drive combined with his liberal thinking to produce a confused social philosophy. The delusion persisted, for only a few weeks before his death, he told Carpenter:

> The blending of social strata in masculine love seems to me to be one of its most pronounced & socially hopeful features. Where it appears, it abolishes class distinctions & opens by a single operation the cataract-bound eye to their futilities.[11]

Unlike Symonds, Carpenter had set out deliberately to escape the bondage of a class that he held responsible for his early maladjustment. His everyday involvement in the socialist movement gave him an affinity with working-class individuals experienced by few from his own class. He found among the Sheffield workers, individuals who shared his political ideals; came to know many of them well, was a familiar visitor to their homes and knew much of their domestic life. In time, he was trusted as a confidant and moved freely and easily from one stratum of life to another.

5

Finding Love

Although there were now friendships in abundance, Carpenter hungered for love. Without an intimate tie his life was incomplete, his powers crippled, his energies misspent. He would write: 'I can hardly bear even now to think of all that early life – to think that until about the age of 37 – I never met with anything like a real satisfaction of the heart'.[1] There had been occasional adventures abroad. On an excursion to Paris one or two of the young prostitutes he passed on the boulevards 'deeply interested' him, but were 'nothing for my need; and I came back to England feeling hopeless and tired out'.[2] There may have been other encounters. He had written in *Towards Democracy*: 'I enter the young prostitute's chamber, where he is arranging the photographs of fashionable beauties and favourite companions and stay with him; we are at ease and understand each other'.[3]

He was not thirty-seven but forty-one when he found his first real satisfaction of the heart. Early in 1886 he was involved in setting up a socialist club in Sheffield, and among the little band of workers was twenty-six-year-old George Hukin, a handsome self-employed razor-grinder. He is lovingly pictured in Carpenter's poem 'In the Stone-floored Workshop', which depicts men dressed in rough clothes, with clogs on their feet and yellow-splashed faces, bent over their grinding-wheels. From the gloom, his work done, emerges,

> a figure with dusty cap and
> Light curls escaping from under it, large dove-grey eyes and
> Dutch-featured face of tears and laughter,
> (So subtle, so rare, so finished a product,)
> A man who understands and accepts all human life and
> character,
> Keen and swift of brain, heart tender and true, and low voice
> Ringing so clear,
> And my dear comrade.[4]

George was a widower, and already courting his soon-to-be second wife, Fannie. Whatever his intimacy with men had been, he had not rejected the advances of the lovesick Carpenter and the friendship quickly became intense. He was soon 'your faithful Chips', and George his 'dear Pippin'.

In the beginning, Hukin struggled to bridge the social gulf between them, confessing:

> I would rather withdraw from, than approach any nearer to you. I feel so mean and little beside you! Altogether unworthy of your friendship. It is not your fault that I feel so. I know you have always tried to put me at my ease, to make me feel at home with you – sorry I cannot [*sic*] come nearer to you. How I should like to yet I feel I can't … Forgive me calling you Mr I know I've offended you often by doing so. I won't do so again I assure you.[5]

In Brighton, 'distributing relics' after the sale of the old family house, Carpenter was cheered to receive an endearing letter from a more confident George:

> You don't know how tempted I feel to come down and join you at Brighton. A thousand thanks for your kind letter. It is so good of you to love me so. I don't think I ever felt as happy in my life as I have felt lately. And I'm sure I love you more than any other friend I have in the world.[6]

The relationship quickly became physical: 'He generally stays the night with me on Saturdays – either at Millthorpe, or at my quarters in Sheffield'.[7] As bed-sharing was not uncommon within working-class families living in overcrowded conditions, Hukin's sleeping with Carpenter would not have been seen as unusual, and in the male-dominated society in which he had been raised, physical contact between men 'was neither frowned upon nor unusual', probably leading Hukin to 'a casual acceptance of sex and companionship between men in private' that did not conflict with sexuality expressed through marriage and fatherhood.[8]

Over Christmas, they spent a week together in London. Back in Sheffield, George could not wait to tell him:

> I think on the whole these have been the happiest Xmas holidays I ever remember, dear old Chips, I don't know what I'd do without you, you are the dearest old Chips on earth. Longing to see you in Sheffield again. Your Dearest Pippin.[9]

Hukin was Carpenter's physical ideal, and almost certainly this was his first consummated love affair. Soon he was spending a great deal of time with George, telling Charles Oates: 'He is staying here for a day or two and tomorrow he and I are going for a 2 or 3 days' walk among the Derbyshire Hills … His love is so disinterested and so tender I hardly dare think it true'.[10] But the relationship on which he seemed to be placing so much store was fated. Carpenter's attentiveness had captivated but smothered Hukin, who was harbouring a secret from his lover. Back in Millthorpe, he revealed that he had asked Fannie to marry him. Charles Oates was in Italy and a crestfallen Carpenter fled to Acqui to be with him, and from where he wrote a consoling letter to a clearly distressed George. 'Your letter has cheered us both up wonderfully … I feel as if quite a load has been taken off me and I hope none of us will ever feel so weighed down again'.[11]

A flurry of letters from Carpenter followed, which brought a confused response from the emotionally torn George, suffering both estrangement and guilt.

> I should like to be with you for just an hour! It seems so very quiet and lonely in this room without you here. I miss you much more than I thought I should and I don't find it so nice, sleeping alone, as I used to think it was … Oh how often I had wanted to tell you about it ever since that first night I slept with you at Millthorpe. You don't know how miserable I have felt all along, just because I wanted to tell you, and yet somehow I was afraid to.[12]

Carpenter, in replying, may have lapsed into self-indulgence. It induced a further despondent reply from George:

> I feel very miserable just now … I think about you and love you more than ever. But I can't bear to think that you are so unhappy, and know that I am the cause of it all … I sometimes feel that I can never bring anything but unhappiness to either you or Fannie and then I feel so miserable that I would like to die. Perhaps it would be best for me then, at least I can't feel as I feel now and live much longer … I don't care what becomes of me, so long as you and Fannie are happy.[13]

An alarmed Carpenter was emollient:

> I have been reading yours of the 24th over more than once and cannot say all I would about it, ah the pain I have put you to, and your goodness. But I will not doubt you any more, or Fannie. I will not really dear George. I will be happy for your sakes as you tell me to be and as I can be now.[14]

The company of handsome Italian men did little to help:

> I got on pretty well with my Italian youth Francesco from Sarona to Genoa but we were both awfully silent, walked for miles without saying a word … I feel my sexual nature swimming. I have been like a monk for the last few weeks![15]

In his head, he had accepted the situation, telling George:

> I do hope now you will be happy. I almost wish you had done me some wrong. I would so gladly forgive you but after all I think you have done the best for us all three … Love and blessings on you and looking forward ever so to seeing you.[16]

George responded: '

> You are so good to forgive me for all the pain I've caused you … you must stay as long as you can and get quite well and strong before you come back'.[17]

Carpenter needed little prompting:

> 'I am glad of an excuse to stay a day or two more as I feel so much better now as if I was getting quite strong again, better than I have felt for a year or two.' But it was not easy to stop thinking about Hukin: 'I could have sworn you were somewhere about

George ... I was walking through the fields, and you came ever so close to me'. And Fannie was now writing to him: 'Another letter from Fannie yesterday ... so good of her'.[18]

He left Acqui for home, and during the journey across the Alps found 'sympathetic' faces in the train. One man, 'an Italian artist I think – was perfectly beautiful. I could have kissed his hands – and would have I think if we had been alone ... a man nearly 40 with black short beard and large perceptive eyes – so tender and warm hearted face, yet not too "refined" but wonderfully well-balanced. How I wished to see him again!'[19]

When George and Fannie married, bizarrely, he bought them a bed as a present and George, still clearly emotionally attached, made an audacious suggestion.

> I do wish you could sleep with us sometimes, Ted, but I don't know whether Fannie would quite like it yet; and I don't feel I could press it on her anyway. Still I often think how nice it would be if we three could only love each other so that we might sleep together sometimes without feeling that there was anything at all wrong in doing so. Dearest Ted, I often think about you – whole days when I'm at work – and there are so many things I think of too that I should like to tell you, and yet I never can.[20]

This was new territory for them all: 'There were no known patterns for their criss-crossing emotions. Yet, somehow, without any maps to guide them they had contained the pain and prevented it from breaking out in ugliness and anger'.[21] Later, he became involved sexually with other men in his socialist circle, 'a startling break with conventional sexual relationships. They were crossing the divides of class, gender and monogamy all at once in the midst of intense political activity, faction fights and anarchist trials'.[22]

His romance with Hukin had united a social purpose in life with the hunger for love that had hunted him down from his earliest days. It was the most enduring and important of all his relationships, and it was Hukin's death that broke his strongest link with the North. The deep attachment that existed between them, long after their brief affair had ended, is revealed in his tenderly beautiful poem '*Philoläus to Diocles*'. It contains the lines:

> All the sweet noons and moons we have spent together;
> All the glad interchange of laughter and love,
> And thoughts, so grave, or fanciful:
> What can compare with these, or what surpass them?
> All the unbroken faith and steadfast reliance,
> nigh twenty years twining the roots of life far down;
> And not a mistrustful hour between us, or moment of anger.[23]

Carpenter had set out deliberately to escape the bondage of a class that he held responsible for his early maladjustment. His everyday involvement in the socialist movement gave him an affinity with working-class individuals experienced by few from his own class. When he found fleeting sexual fulfilment with Hukin, it was with an individual who was a model of self-improvement; an individual who, in spite of his initial feelings of inferiority, he regarded as an equal. But the affair brought home to him how finding his kind of love would be a life-long struggle; a 'fierce and frightful waging for a mate and the mockery of women always thrust in the way ...'[24] He felt the need to close ranks; there had to be solidarity among lovers of their own sex. He told Charles Oates:

> We are going to form by degrees a body of friends, who will be tied together by the strongest general bond, and also by personal attachments – and that we shall help each other immensely by the mutual support we shall be able to give to each other. The

knowledge that there are many others in the same position as oneself will remove that sense of loneliness which one feels so keenly at times – especially when plunged in the society of the Philistines – and which is really almost unbearable.[25]

Later, the idea of a special attachment between homosexual men inspired a small circle of Carpenter's young Cambridge friends. One of the most prominent was twenty-one-year-old Charles Ashbee. When at Millthorpe, he was dismayed by the mass production of the Sheffield cutlery 'sweat shops' shown to him by Carpenter. It planted in him the desire for the restoration of true craftsmanship, leading him to become a prime instigator in the Arts and Crafts movement. Ashbee had accepted his own sexual affinities, having fallen in love with the artist Roger Fry, a fellow undergraduate, but not homosexual. When Carpenter visited them in Cambridge, they felt his personal magnetism, Ashbee confiding in his journal that being near him, 'has elated us and drawn us out of ourselves into another world, another cycle of feeling.'[26] His eyes had been opened to the homosexual demi-monde and a daring idea of fraternity seems to have been sown by Carpenter. 'He unfolded to me a wonderful idea of his of a new free-masonry, a comradeship in the life of men which might be based on our little Cambridge circle of friendships'. He seemed to sense that this might be more than a clandestine society, asking himself: 'Are we to be the nucleus out of which the new Society is to be organised'?[27]

This youthful idealisation would never go beyond a drawing together through the strengthening of personal attachments. Although Carpenter had only fleetingly visualised a community of men united by their same-sex desires, by the 1890s, the impulse to turn inwards prevailed in English homosexual circles, in the form of the *Order of Chaeronea*. It took its name from the battle of Chaeronea, in which the Theban band of male lovers died together fighting the Macedonians. It was established by

George Cecil Ives, to further what he called 'the Cause'. Its high-minded ideals were marked by initiation ceremonies and rituals. It did its work out of the glare of public scrutiny, drawing in educated homosexuals, who could only enter into its intrigues through the personal recommendation of an existing member. No records of its membership or activities were kept. If working-class individuals made good bed-partners it is unlikely that any were ever admitted to its ranks. In truth, it was a gathering of cultured individuals sharing a sexual ethos that blended Platonic and Whitmanic ideas. 'Obsessed with secrecy and his work for the Cause, Ives was a prude and a puritan'.[28]

Carpenter is not known to have been a member, but by this time he had moved decisively away from clandestine association towards an open defence of same-sex love; one in which the homosexual was to have 'a fitting place and sphere of usefulness in the general scheme of society'.[29]

6

A Rogue Intervention

In the autumn of 1884, as Carpenter was settling into his new life at Millthorpe, events were unfolding in London that would result in the criminalisation of all homosexual acts in England for eighty-two years. But the train of events that led to an extension of the law governing sexual relations between men did not begin as a concerted campaign against homosexuality. For more than two years attempts had been made to introduce legislation to revise the law concerning a number of female-related sexual offences, including child prostitution. In May 1884, a bill for this purpose had, for the second time, stalled in the House of Commons.

In July, the *Pall Mall Gazette* published a four-part report under the title 'The Maiden Tribute of Modern Babylon', which sent the circulation of the paper soaring. Written by the editor, William Stead, its purpose was to expose the widespread traffic in young girls. He showed how easy it was to procure girls for sex by 'abducting' the thirteen-year-old daughter of an East End chimney sweep. Although his action was intended to expose this traffic, the law took a different view and Stead found himself serving a short prison sentence. But the outcry that followed his revelations forced the government to hastily resume the passage of the bill, intended, *inter alia*, to raise the age of female consent to sexual intercourse from thirteen to sixteen. The draft legislation went before the House of Commons on the sixth of August.

In London, female prostitution was the most visible manifestation of unrestrained male lust. Henry Mayhew, in his *London Labour and the London Poor*, estimated that over a thousand prostitutes were walking the streets there in the 1880s. Members strolling to the House that evening, had they cared to look, could not have avoided seeing young males plying the same trade in the bustling Haymarket, or the seductive soldier-prostitute parading in all his finery along London's leafy park-walks. Only the previous year an extensive homosexual ring had been uncovered in Dublin Castle, the seat of the British Government in Ireland, when harsh sentences for sodomy were handed down. Widespread homosexuality among boys in public schools and its diffusion into the upper reaches of society had also become a fixation. If female prostitution was the most manifest symptom of unrestrained male lust, indecency between men, and the corrupting of youths by men, were equally condemned. At a time when the idea of a stable homosexual relationship was unthinkable, the homosexual was portrayed as a self-centred egoist and woman-hater.

Had Henry Labouchère, the Liberal Member of Parliament for Northampton, perished under the wheels of a carriage as he made his way to the House that evening, homosexual law reform in England may have taken an entirely different course. At the time, any homosexual activity between men was dealt with under the laws against sodomy; all other sexual acts between males being treated by the law as preparatory to the act of anal intercourse and deemed to be attempted sodomy. Late at night, in a depleted House of Commons, it did not take much to persuade those present that this was an opportunity to extend the law on sex between men. By the end of the debate on the intended legislation, Labouchère had succeeded in having a five-line clause on homosexuality inserted into the bill. It read:

> Any male person who, in public or private, commits, or is a party to the commission of, or procures or attempts to procure the commission by any male person, of any act of gross indecency with another male person, shall be guilty of a misdemeanour, and being convicted thereof, shall be liable, at the discretion of the court, to be imprisoned for any term not exceeding one year with or without hard labour.

Labouchère, allegedly, had intended that the penalty should be much more severe, ranging from seven years with hard labour to life imprisonment. But the House was content with the classification of the offence as a *misdemeanour* and the extension of the sentence to a maximum of two years, with or without hard labour. The subject of homosexuality itself, was never debated and the amendment became section 11, 'Outrages to Public Decency', of the Criminal Law Amendment Act, 1885. It did not replace the 1861 Offences against the Person Act, which retained buggery as a *criminal* offence.

The amendment was entirely at Labouchère's initiative, as the government had no plans to introduce legislation on homosexuality at this time. At the behest of one man, in one stroke a seemingly innocuous paragraph, for the first time in English law made all forms of male homosexual behaviour a prosecutable offence, where it could not be proved that the accused had engaged in anal intercourse.

The clause was not a model of drafting precision. The introduction of the catch-all term 'gross indecency' made any physical activity between males, deemed to be sexual, an indictable offence; leaving the *nature* of the supposed offence to be determined entirely by judges or juries. More fundamentally, the amendment made gross indecency an offence whether committed in a public or a private place. The practice under the buggery laws had always been to prosecute homosexual acts wherever committed, but to incorporate this in legislation marked a historic change in the reach of the law, at a time when the sovereignty of the individual over purely self-regarding actions was being asserted.

The legislation would remain in force until the Sexual Offences Act of 1967 decriminalised sexual acts in private between two consenting adults over the age of twenty-one, but in England and Wales only.[1] This was in stark contrast to homosexual law reform on the European continent. In France, under the *Code Napoléon*, sexual relations between consenting males that did not involve violence, corrupt minors or outrage public decency, had been legal since 1792. By 1889, when Italy introduced a similar law, the Netherlands, Belgium and Spain had all introduced comparable legislation.

7

—

The Making of a Socialist

The 1880s was a highly significant phase in Carpenter's personal development, his emotional life, and, importantly, his movement towards the articulation of a critical sexual politics and the defence of homosexuality. The decade saw a new phase in working-class agitation, with demands for a living wage, union representation and parliamentary and franchise reforms. Recurrent large-scale unemployment and widespread poverty raised awareness and pricked consciences, drawing into political activity middle and upper-class individuals like Carpenter. They formed a new intelligentsia morally repelled by the spectacle of brutalising work, social fragmentation and the spoliation of the environment. Some electoral and trade union reforms had been introduced, but many had lost faith in the capacity of the then Liberal Party to meet the aspirations of the working-classes and were turning to more radical alternatives. Although, as yet, Carpenter had no 'definite conception' of how economic change and social reconstruction could be brought about, for several years, 'in a vague form', his ideas had become socialistic. His Cambridge sermons, if hedged about with anxiety over the danger of unfettered workers' demands, had clearly been infused by such ethical ideals.

He had arrived in the north in 1874, but it was nine years before he entered the public arena of politics, marked by the publication of *Towards Democracy*. He soon found himself caught up in a 'great new tide of human life', which acted as 'an extraordinary inspiration and encouragement.' He came into contact with socialists and anarchists, feminists and suffragists, the trades unions and non-conformist religious groups. In time, he would know and work with many of the leading representatives of these groups. He likened them to so many streams flowing into a great river and felt that 'something massive must surely emerge from it all'. And he found, 'a wonderful enthusiasm and belief in a new ideal of fraternity'.[1]

The first public expression of his allegiance to the socialist movement came in a lecture to a large audience in Sheffield's Hall of Science on 18 March 1883. The subject of this, in his own words, 'semi-socialist' lecture, *co-operative production*, was topical at a time when alternative forms of industrial organisation were being advocated by radicals. 'Go into any factory in Sheffield and you will find depressed faces, stunted sickly forms, dirt, polluted air, hurried bad work'. What pleasure was there in work 'making 1000 house-nails a day'? Meanwhile, 'the Capitalist winks at bad work so long as it sells and pays scandal wages'.[2]

He had found his public voice and the next seven years saw the appearance of some of his most widely read political and social tracts; his contented life at Millthorpe spawning a succession of polemical articles and pamphlets. All, he would claim, contained 'theories or views which flowed 'perfectly logically from the central idea of *Towards Democracy*.'[3] A typical example, was a humorous parody of bourgeois existence; the sorrows of the 'well-to-do', of a class shut off from 'the great stream of human life'; confined in their 'prison houses of futility', their 'desirable mansions'.[4] When this was republished in 1887 with other pieces, in *England's Ideal*, a reviewer for the *Pall Mall Gazette* suggested that they 'should have been got up luxuriously, and offered at half a guinea, for they are specially addressed to the rich'. He was, to distinguish himself as a pricker of the conscience of a dominant class trapped in 'a jungle of idiotic duties' and 'thin-lipped respectabilities'; alienated from the vast majority of the population. Although he would acquire a reputation as a *maker* of socialists, much energy was directed towards *unmaking* the bourgeois mind; towards redeeming the class from which he had sprung. 'I know that even in the midst of all these shackles and impediments, that wonderfulest of things, the human soul, may work out its own salvation'.[5] This was to become a characteristic of much of his political writing; setting him apart from the many in the socialist movement who spoke firstly to the 'slumbering masses'. Carpenter never ceased to address those whom he saw as the perpetrators of their oppression, his own class; the people he knew best. The memory of his father's constant struggle to maintain the family's economic survival, his mother's ingrained acquiescence to the values of respectability and gentility, and his own forced participation in the conventions of his class all combined to elicit a distinctive political critique. And if, as Edith Ellis would observe, he sometimes appeared 'to be almost sentimentally lenient to the sinner',[6] it was because it was this class above all which had to change; had to accept the moral ideal of a common life.

In the same year he published a pamphlet, *Modern Money-Lending and the Meaning of Dividends*.[7] In venturing to write on such a topic he was conscious that he was himself the son of a *rentier* and, indeed, was himself a *rentier*. In addition to his own interest-earning investments – he owned a considerable number of railway company shares inherited from his father – he occasionally loaned money to members of his family, receiving small sums in interest. But he believed that a real distinction could be drawn between 'legitimate interest and odious usury'.

The following year he wrote *England's Ideal*, a further scathing attack on the mode of life of the monied class, whose principal aim was 'to live dependent on others, consuming much and creating next to nothing'. It was a class that lived in 'unproductive wastefulness', whilst a vaster class 'sank down into the abyss of toil, penury and degradation'.[8] More articles and pamphlets in similar vein followed. He wrote two trenchant pieces, *The Cause of Poverty*,[9] and, *Social Progress and Individual Effort,*[10] both repeating the argument that had become a central theme of his politics: institutional changes were secondary to personal transformation; the foundation on which his own adult life was built. As, again, Edith Ellis remarked, looking back on his entry into the political world: '[He] began to realise that no cleric, no middle-class idler, no conventional philanthropist, no mere self-seeker or maxim-maker, and no sincere person, can radically alter institutions till they have altered themselves'.[11] All these pieces steadily earned him a reputation as a new voice and a trenchant critic of the existing order. Writing apart, he was lecturing up and down the country on a variety of subjects. In 1887, the piece *England's Ideal* was used as the title for what soon became a popular collection of several of these earlier papers and articles, going through nine editions and remaining in print for over thirty years.[12]

In early 1889 he risked controversy when he published an article with the title *Civilisation: Its Cause and Cure*.[13] It contained echoes of his undergraduate essay *On the Continuance of Modern Civilisation*. For the Victorians, *their* 'civilisation' was the highpoint of human progress, but Carpenter argued that the commercial, industrial capitalist period, marked by the private ownership of property, was a 'temporary alienation from true life'; a distinct stage in social evolution destined to be succeeded by a later stage. In the same year, he combined this and other articles and papers in book form, under the *Modern Civilisation* title.[14] The most contentious was a criticism of modern science. He had been steeped in mathematics and the physical sciences at Cambridge and had been lecturing on astronomy and the history of science. But now a reaction set in and he questioned the primacy given to science by the radical intelligentsia. A belief in the transformative power of scientific knowledge ran deep in the veins of most socialists, eager to apply its methods to eradicate the numerous imperfections of society. He shocked a good many of his mathematical and scientific friends, who accused him of being blind to modern progress, of preferring ignorance to intelligence and of desiring a return to the state of primitive man. But, by now, Carpenter was an unapologetic *ethical* socialist, convinced that more than the application of reason was needed when it came to changing society. He had already written in *England's Ideal*: 'Do not be misled to suppose that science and the intellect are or can be the source of social progress or change. It is the moral births and outgrowths that originate, science and the intellect only give form to these.'[15]

Although his socialist beliefs were firmly rooted in the language at the heart of *Towards Democracy*, he found inspiration for his allegiance to the socialist cause in two contemporary works. In 1879, Henry George, an American economist and social critic, had published a lengthy analysis of industrial capitalism under the title *Progress and Poverty*.[16] For George, progress with poverty was the great enigma of the times. The source of the unequal distribution of wealth was the institution of private property in land, and so long as this existed no increase in productive power could permanently benefit the masses. This highly controversial book quickly crossed the Atlantic and had an immediate impact on the formation of socialist thinking. It was an intellectual bridge over which many passed on the journey from liberal individualism to socialism. George Bernard Shaw's own conversion had come at a meeting addressed by George during the ruinous 'rack-rent' impositions in Ireland. Shaw bought a copy from a steward and 'devoured it with the intensest interest'.[17]

In George's tract there was extensive reference to Malthus, frequent mention of J. S. Mill but not a single mention of Marx. This was soon remedied in a work by Henry Mayers Hyndman. Hyndman, from a wealthy upper-class family and educated at Eton and Cambridge, had stood unsuccessfully as a Conservative parliamentary candidate in the 1870s. In 1881, he took an ideological step to the left, after he had read a French edition of Marx's *Capital*. Convinced of the truth of the Marxian analyses, he produced a small booklet, *England for All*,[18] in which he borrowed liberally from Marx. He then founded a new political grouping, the Democratic Federation, which became a magnet for all kinds of political veterans. At its inaugural meeting he presented copies of his booklet to the assembled, claiming that it, and a second work by him, *Historical Basis of Socialism*, were the first expositions of *scientific* socialism to be published in England. With a flowing white beard, dressed in frock coat and top hat, he cut a bizarre figure as he proclaimed to working-class audiences that Marx was the Aristotle of the nineteenth century.

Before Carpenter read *England for All*, his ideas had lacked the 'definite outline' so necessary for action. Hyndman's account of the brutal operation of the industrial system rang true with what he had found and strengthened his conviction that such an order was doomed. In particular, Hyndman's chapter on Marx's theory of surplus value was decisive: 'The instant I read that chapter ... the mass of floating impressions, sentiments, ideals, etc., in my mind fell into shape – and I had a clear line of social reconstruction before me'.[19] On a visit to London, he dropped in on a committee meeting of the Federation, where he found 'a group of conspirators sitting'. Hyndman was in the chair and those gathered around the table included William Morris and several individuals who would become influential in the promotion of the socialist cause. Carpenter did not join the Federation (later to be renamed the Social Democratic Federation) but in a singular act of generosity donated the considerable sum of £300 to help launch a fire-eating weekly paper, *Justice*. Hyndman and others, but not Carpenter, sold it down Fleet Street and the Strand, greeted by the 'respectables' with mixed alarm and amusement:

> Morris in his soft hat and blue suit, Campion, Frost and Joynes in the morning garments of the well-to-do, several workingmen comrades, and I myself wearing the new frock coat in which Shaw said I was born, with a tall hat and good gloves, all earnestly engaged in selling a penny Socialist paper during the busiest time of the day in London's busiest thoroughfare.[20]

Carpenter's financial largesse towards the infant SDF earned him a single mention in Hyndman's autobiography, where the ambiguous reference to 'our friend Carpenter' more than hints that he always regarded him as marginal to the cause. He had made it perfectly clear that he had little time for persons of Carpenter's frame of mind, once telling Shaw: 'I do not want the movement to be a depository of old cranks, humanitarians, vegetarians, anti-vivisectionists, arty-crafties and all the rest of them. We are scientific socialists and have no room for sentimentalists'.[21]

In turn, Carpenter had no time for the 'theory-mongers' who believed fervently in revolutions; bourgeois dilettantes masquerading as the 'representatives' of the working-class. He also had a visceral distrust of authoritarian personalities like Hyndman. At every crisis in the industrial situation during the 1880s, Hyndman was certain that the millennium was at hand; that the Democratic Federation would resolve itself into a Committee of Public Safety, and that it would then be for him, as Chairman, 'to guide the Ship of State into the calm haven of Socialism'![22] Hyndman was confident that 1889, the centenary of the French Revolution, would see an uprising in England but it passed with nothing more effectual than the Socialist Congress in Paris, at which a great deal of disagreement on both means and ends was evident. Later, Hyndman expressed the same hope during the imperialist turmoil of 1899, which only gave birth to the Boer War. He had an extraordinary gift for falling out with his socialist friends, and finally led the SDF into the wilderness, to join the long line of English sectarian bodies whose members were destined to remain on the periphery of the political world.

If many individuals like Carpenter rejected the canonical status given to Marx's political economy, they could still accept key parts of his economic and social analysis. Marxist ideas, which were then as novel to him as they were to many others, helped him to find his feet in the swirling waters of socialist rhetoric. He, too, had read the French edition of *Capital*, and thought it was self-evident that the *surplus value* created by the labouring classes was the bedrock of the lives of the rentier class. The labour theory of value had also been strongly supported in his 1885 pamphlet *Modern Money-Lending and the Meaning of Dividends*. He also accepted a second Marxian proposition: that, from age to age, the laws represented the code of the dominant or ruling class: in his own time commercialism and its distinctive watchword property. When the ideal of society was possession, the object of its special condemnation was the thief: 'You may beat your wife within an inch of her life and only get three months; but if you steal a rabbit, you may be "sent" for years'.[23]

Without subscribing to the inevitability of the overthrow of the capitalist system, he thought that industrial reorganisation would come, almost of necessity, to prevent a collapse of the system. 'The first serious disturbance now and the wheels will actually cease to go round', he wrote in *England's Ideal*. But on the critical issue of *causation*, he rejected outright historical materialism. Ideals were the main factors in any nation's progress. They, ultimately, decided the direction of its movement. In

England's Ideal there would not be a single quotation from the Gospel of St Marx.

William Morris was equally opposed to collectivist state socialism. His membership of the Democratic Federation, daily rubbing shoulders with the doctrinaire Hyndman, was bound to be short-lived. At the end of his tether over the political machinations in London, he visited Carpenter at Millthorpe. Its tranquillity, after the continuous factionalism in London, induced a murmur of regret:

> I listened with longing heart to his account of his patch of ground, seven acres: he says that he and his fellow can almost live on it: they grow their own wheat, and send flowers and fruit to Chesterfield and Sheffield markets; all that sounds very agreeable to me … a refuge from our mean squabbles and corrupt society; but I am too old now, even if it were not dastardly to desert.[24]

But, barely a week after returning home, he broke away from the Federation to set up the Socialist League, ominously, taking an anarchist faction with him. The rupture spelled danger for Carpenter, always the reconciler. In a hard-hitting piece for *The Clarion*, he knocked heads together:

> Such a big thing it is – and it is going to be – such innumerable work to be done, and of all sorts, of all kinds. Burns at his kind, Keir Hardie at his, Nanquam [Robert Blatchford] at another, Morris and Kropotkin at another, and the unknown equally important workers each at theirs. Criticise each other's work by all means, but don't make the mistake of thinking that because the other man is working at a different part of the same building from you, that therefore he is working in opposition to you. Don't go and kick the hodman's ladder down because you are not going to use the bricks which he is bringing up.[25]

After anarchists gained control of the Socialist League, a despairing Morris withdrew from the fray; confiding to Carpenter that he had spent a great part of his working life designing furniture, wall-paper, carpets and curtains, but had come to regard this work, for which he was renowned, as 'mostly rubbish.' Probably recollecting his visits to Millthorpe, he expressed a preference for living 'with the plainest whitewashed walls and wooden chairs and tables'.[26]

As argued, morality, not science, was the foundation of Carpenter's socialism. The ethical imperative of personal transformation he had found exemplified by members of the Fellowship of the New Life, which met for the first time in London in October 1883. Members wanted to see fundamental social and economic changes, while recognising that changing themselves; aspiring to be better people, was equally important. There was also an added appeal for Carpenter, in the emphasis that members placed on the *spirituality* rather than the *physicality* of love. It was a milieu in which he could be less guarded about his sexuality. Although he was not a founding member, when in London he might attend a meeting and would give the occasional lecture. Importantly, it was through the Fellowship that he came to know Havelock Ellis and Olive Schreiner.

Ellis had been attending a meeting of the Fellowship, when a youth sitting next to him put a small book into his hands. It was *Towards Democracy*. He thumbed through a few pages and returned it with the remark, 'Whitman and water'. When he came across a copy on a bookstall, he thought it 'might be worthwhile to rescue it'. Reading it at leisure, he found that it was 'a genuinely original book full of inspiring and beautiful and consoling things'. It appealed to his 'youthful impulse of revolt against the existing social order'. [27]

He first came face-to-face with Carpenter at a Fellowship meeting. The proceedings were already under way when, sitting with his back to the door, he heard it being opened quietly. 'I turned round for a moment and saw two brightly gleaming eyes out of the background of a quietly humorous face. In that first swift glance, as will sometimes happen, I gained a more vivid picture of Edward Carpenter's characteristic face than in all the long years I knew him afterwards. [28] It was the beginning of a life-long friendship.

Although self-transformation was Carpenter's personal ideal, he *always grappled* with the here and now, and it was the here and now that he wished to see *humanised*. For decades, he would continue to lecture widely on very practical topics to trade union branches, socialist societies, non-conformist churches, ethical societies, fledgling Independent Labour Party groups, and Fabian and Humanitarian League branches. These lectures ranged in scope from mundane issues about small-holdings and allotments to the grander possibilities of 'non-governmental society'. Lectures on the need to humanise work, to tame the free market and its destructive social relations, and to abolish private ownership of the means of production, were interspersed with others as diverse as industrial pollution and vivisection.

To use the term 'making socialists' is the best way to describe his role in the movement. Many individuals who were to become prominent in its history would testify to his influence. *Towards Democracy* became a kind of bible for many youthful socialists, who would revere Carpenter as one of the movement's founding fathers. His popular and widely read political tracts were not works of abstruse theory but down-to-earth essays, written with literary power and freshness of style; carried along by irony and humour. He had developed a charming, non-bombastic writing style; one that had some of the characteristics of a homily but without strident moralising.

As a socialist, he wanted to change the distribution of economic and political power, but equally, he wanted to change gender relationships and attitudes towards human sexuality. The latter two would become integral parts of his socialist creed, but, as we explore below, in writing so prominently on human sexuality he would attract hostility from fellow socialists. He was convinced that changes in gender relationships and sexual attitudes and behaviour would form part of the transformative power of socialism. But his linking of sexual reform with a vision of a new social order disturbed a number of the movement's leading figures, who considered it to be a dangerous distraction from the cause. Many also held conservative views on the role of women and the sexual division of labour, believing that there were limits to such advances, fixed by the physical constitution of women and the necessary societal differentiation of gender roles. Many did not accept that all distinctions in social functions between men and women, beyond the physical fact of child-bearing, should be open to examination. Gender and sex concerns, it was argued, if pushed forward would be rejected by the public. Such questions had to remain subordinate to economic and political reorganisation, and any attempt to fasten such ideas to socialist propaganda would be damaging.

The then conventional socialist view on sexuality was typically expressed by Robert Blatchford, editor of the influential popular paper *The Clarion*. Blatchford accepted that relations between the sexes were 'all wrong now' but insisted that consideration of such issues had to come *after* economic and industrial change. Public prejudice was so strong on these matters that if socialists were identified with such radical reforms it would seriously impede their work:

> I think that the accomplishment of the industrial change will need all our energy and will consume all the years we are likely to live ... If so, if Socialism is not established during our lives, or only at the end of our lives, and if a state of Socialism must necessarily precede the change in the sexual relations, it follows that the sexual change will not concern us personally;

but only concern the next generation ... In short, I think the time is not ripe for Socialists, *as* Socialists, to meddle with the sexual question.[29]

When the fourth, most homoerotic, and most autobiographical part of *Towards Democracy* appeared in 1902, Blatchford, who had liked earlier parts, turned against it, complaining that Carpenter should not 'effront us by echoes of Walt Whitman's lubberly frankness about sex'.[30] Edward's friend Bruce Glasier also recorded in his diary that he found such 'celebration of sexual sensation' difficult to stomach, strongly abhorring 'orgiastic literature'.[31] Clearly, for many, to advocate both socialism and homosexual love was a double-jeopardy. Whatever appreciation there would be for Carpenter's women-related pamphlets, the subject of homosexuality was taboo. George Bernard Shaw was certain that 'No movement could survive association with such propaganda'.[32]

Some of the 'constitutional' suffragists also distanced themselves, not wanting their cause to be muddled up in the public mind with sexual liberation. But for Carpenter, the sexual degradation of women and child prostitution were inextricably linked to the widespread acceptance of unfettered male self-expression and power. Whatever institutional reforms were introduced, no real change in social relations could be achieved whilst behaviour which dehumanised half the population was condoned.

Of all the individuals within the mid-eighties coterie of socialists the most adamantly opposed to almost all feminist, suffragist and 'new women' claims was E. Belfort Bax, a founding member of the Social Democratic Federation. But, although implacably opposed to the women-related reforms that Carpenter will advocate, he was one of the few socialists who supported him on the issue of homosexual freedom. Only consent and the absence of coercion were relevant issues. Non-procreative sexual acts were legitimate and concerned only the welfare of the individuals concerned. 'Every human being has a complete ethical right to the physical exercise of his or her sexual instinct.'[33] Sexual acts belonged to the sphere of aesthetics, not ethics. To be brought within the sphere of ethics they had to be connected with a distinct social relation outside the persons immediately concerned. Otherwise, they were *self-regarding* actions.[34]

In some quarters, antipathy to Carpenter's sexual writings would never disappear. The straight-talking George Orwell (Eric Blair) would complain of 'eunuch types with a vegetarian smell who go about spreading sweetness and light ... readers of Edward Carpenter or some other pious sodomites talking with BBC accents'.[35] And again, in *The Road to Wigan Pier,* he railed against the disquieting prevalence of cranks, wherever socialists were gathered together: 'One sometimes gets the impression that the mere words "Socialism" "Communism" draw towards them with magnetic force every fruit-juice drinker, nudist, sandal-wearer, sex-maniac, "Nature Cure" quack, pacifist and feminist in England'.[36]

PART TWO

8

The Woman Question

In 1881, twenty-six-year-old Olive Schreiner arrived in England from the then Cape Province, with the ambition to become a doctor. Not having the funds to cover the long period of study required, she would twice begin training as a nurse, but the chronic asthma that would plague her for the whole of her life would make this impossible. She had brought with her the text of a novel, written under a *nom-de-plume*, for which she had been unable to find a publisher in the Cape. Here, it was eventually accepted by Chapman and Hall, with the title *The Story of an African Farm*. There was consternation in the publisher's office when a small girlish figure appeared and announced herself as Ralph Irons.

The subject of the novel, the 'woman question', was to become the compelling passion of her life. Full of magical pictures of life and nature on the African karoo, the idyllic title masked its real subject: the helplessness and humiliation of its heroine, who rejected her pre-ordained life and prayed for the day when 'to be born a woman will not be to be born branded'.

It sold well, and after two further issues her name appeared as the author. Although it was not widely reviewed, its significance was recognised in London's radical circles and Schreiner found herself feted as the author of a novel destined to have a circulation across three continents. It opened up a new life.

One of the individuals keen to know her was Havelock Ellis. During the close friendship that developed, he passed her his copy of Carpenter's *Towards Democracy*. She was quick to tell him: 'I have been reading the little book you lent me all the afternoon. I like it, and I like it more the more I read it, and when I re-read a page or two I like it better than at first. It is true, and it expresses what is in our hearts, ours of to-day'.[1]

In turn, Carpenter had read *An African Farm* 'with great interest, much of it more than once', as he told Ellis: '[It] is original and there is much feeling and poetic power in it. Give my kind regards to the authoress when you see her'.[2] It was at a gathering of members of the Fellowship of the New Life that he noticed 'a charming girl-face, of *riant* Italian type' smiling across at him. It was the beginning of a close, loving, and, for Carpenter, life-changing friendship. He was at once struck by her 'wonderful beauty and vivacity … fine eyes … resolute yet mobile mouth', all set in 'a determined little square-set body'. And he would soon feel the force of her 'lightning-quick mind'.[3] She was the antithesis of the 'lady' of his own parodies. He could not help contrasting such a vibrant open personality with the cramped lives of his sisters, frittering away their talents in genteel pastimes, their elemental needs unacknowledged and unfulfilled.

The brooding discontent that Schreiner harboured at having been born a female in a world in which women were subordinated, propelled her towards men who would treat her, not as a woman, but as an equal and a fellow-worker, without her sex ever intruding. The awareness of how much more life would have given her as a man was never far from the surface. She would complain: 'I wish I was a man that I might be friends with all of you, but you know my sex must always divide'.[4] If the gender divide could never be closed, Carpenter was one of the few men who treated her 'as a worker and not as a woman'.[5] There would be a special bond between them; the women stereotype of the day imprisoned Schreiner and, equally, Carpenter was imprisoned by the prevailing stereotype of the masculine male. As their friendship moved from polite acquaintanceship to intimacy, she poured out her hopes and fears in long heart-felt letters. They revealed a complex, troubled individual subject to chronic, near-suicidal depression, often feeling persecuted by others; grieving for the suffering of humankind, craving love but finding personal relationships difficult. Beneath her merry-seeming exterior, he saw a vein of 'ineradicable pessimism': 'Edward, do you know I am beginning to see our Socialist movement much more clearly … And at the same time, I have a feeling stronger than ever before of the mystery and insolubility of things. What little tiny children we are and what *does* it mean?'[6]

At the very time of their first meeting, he was falling in love with George Hukin, and it was Schreiner who, setting aside her own romantic entanglements, helped him through the dark days that followed after the relationship ended. She would see only one future for him: 'Edward you must write much. Make your life consist in that. You and I must have no personality. We must die whilst yet we live … We must work, and every time our heart pains us work – till the agony gets still'.[7]

Questions of sex and questions of politics would always be entwined in Schreiner's struggle to give artistic expression to her ideas: 'The question of sex is so very *complex*, and you cannot treat it adequately at all unless you show its complexity'. In moments of weakness, she was inclined to leave the sex question and turn to other problems that were always drawing her. But she could not turn away from the work that she felt to be her 'own', although it would 'be as if a great iron weight had rolled off me if I had once said what I have to say'.[8]

She would craft novels in which the people of her imagination became more real than those of flesh and blood, and through them she applied her moral code. The allegorical story became her medium, but it would be many years before she came close to saying all she had to say, politically, in *Women and Labour*, published in 1911. The artistic portrayal of female suppression, which she was struggling with when she wrote this, remained the 'great iron weight' for the rest of her life. Her last novel, *From Man to Man*, was not published until six years after her death. Concerned with white women's confinement in domesticity, it also embraced the lives of black women and girls, in the context of the racism and sexism of the times, in both South Africa and England.

In 1885, a group led by the socialist intellectual and eugenicist Karl Pearson set up the Men and Women's Club, when Schreiner became a member of the executive committee. It was exclusive, with an upper limit of twenty persons, divided equally between men and women. Although some women members objected to the almost exclusive focus on women as 'the problem', with little attention given to the male, Pearson gained Schreiner's allegiance after he read the opening paper, *The Woman's Question*. It was a comprehensive examination of the numerous 'social and sexualogical problems' which surrounding it. The disregard for such issues, he argued, made much of the talk emanating from the women's rights' platforms superficial and unconvincing. Rhetorical flourishes of 'justice' and of 'right' carried little weight with the cerebral Pearson. The lack of such investigations diminished much of what, earlier, John Stuart Mill and Mary Wollstonecraft had written on the woman question. (Pearson had resisted the wish of some members to name the club after Wollstonecraft.) Women could not be fully free unless they gained a position of political and social influence equal to men's, he argued. Complete emancipation for women meant 'a revolutionary change in social habits and sexual ideals'.[9]

Carpenter did not become a member of the Club, but warmed to Pearson after Schreiner urged him to read his *Sex and Socialism*, in which, like Carpenter, he coupled the socialist movement with the movement for the liberation of women: 'The first steps towards our ideal are the spread of Socialism and the complete emancipation of our sisters', Pearson wrote.[10] The socialist and the advocate of women's rights were fighting the same battle, but Pearson went much further than the advocates of franchise reform: 'The sex-relation of the future will not be regarded as a union for the birth of children, but as the closest form of friendship between man and woman. Thus, one of the chief causes of woman's economic dependence will disappear. Her sex-relationship will not habitually connote sex-dependence'.[11] Socialism was not a mere scheme of political change. It was a new morality and one inseparable from the 'woman question'.

9

A Defence of Erotic Life

Carpenter absorbed many of the advanced ideas about women that arose from the debates within the Men and Women's Club, and from Pearson's work. In 1893, he began to write a number of pamphlets on 'sex-questions', although not questions that lay strictly in the domain of 'sexology', those 'fanciful divisions and dissections of human nature'.[1] From the very beginning, his purpose in writing on human sexuality *was* ethical: to challenge deeply entrenched attitudes towards the expression of the 'sex-passion' and to raise questions which were 'generally tabooed and practically not discussed at all.'[2] Of the few men who at this time supported the reform of sexual codes, he was the most persistent in addressing specific problems underlying relationships between the sexes and, at a deeper level, the modes of expression of the sexual instinct. Homosexual love, if personally the most urgent, was only one dimension of human sexuality.

When he began to compose these ground-breaking tracts, the problems of economic and social transformation, the predicament of women, and the plight of the homosexual had become closely interconnected. We do not know what consideration he gave to this possibly personally damaging departure from what, up to then, had been his conventional socialist writings, but this decision dramatically changed the direction of his life and public profile. He would certainly have recognised the strategic advantage of establishing himself as a writer on sexual issues before, as he intended, turning to the discussion of homosexuality. He had established connections with women's reform groups, and that a number of leading feminists were his friends provided a legitimising context. And, as a man, he could say things, particularly about male dominance, which coming from a woman would have been easily dismissed.

So important did he hold these issues to be, that he had tried to persuade Schreiner and other of his women friends to take up the subject. In the summer of 1893, Schreiner spent several months in a rented cottage close to Millthorpe, and other 'advanced' women friends who were there during the summer included Kate Salt, the wife of Henry Salt, and Katherine Conway, who had just married the prominent socialist Bruce Glasier. Olive came over frequently, and with such progressive women in the house, issues surrounding their sex were likely to have figured in many of their conversations. But Carpenter failed to convince one of them to take the subject up, 'so [I] had to deal with it myself'.[3] Over the next year he produced three inter-related pamphlets: *Sex-Love, and its Place in a Free Society*; *Woman, and Her Place in a Free Society*; and *Marriage in a Free Society*. A fourth pamphlet, *Man the Ungrown*, was also written. He knew that he would have no chance with ordinary publishers, so they were printed and distributed by The Labour Press Society of Manchester, which had been set up with financial support from Carpenter to spread socialist ideas.

The first three pamphlets covered a range of issues, including male supremacy, on which Victorian sexual conventions rested, the social degradation of women, the burden of child-bearing, motherhood and prostitution. Each had a clear, unambiguous aim: to challenge Victorian gender and sexual orthodoxies, and to initiate a discussion on the healthiness of the expression of sexual energy. They were also an attack on the prevailing economic and social subservience of women. The fourth pamphlet condemned the Victorian male attitudes that perpetuated women's 'serfdom'. The anger that he felt towards the subjugation of women was expressed in a powerful political statement, which went like a dagger to the heart of Victorian 'manhood':

> ... the male bitten by it [the greed of private property] not only claimed possession of everything he could lay hands upon, but ended by enslaving and appropriating his own mate ... reducing her also to a mere chattel, a slave and a plaything ... shutting her more and more into the seclusion of the boudoir and the harem, or down to the drudgery of the hearth; confining her body, her mind; playing always upon her sex-nature, accentuating always that, as though she was indeed nought else but sex ... arrogating to himself a masculine licence, yet revenging the least unfaithfulness on her part by casting her out into the scorned life of the prostitute; and granting her more and more but one choice in life – to be a free woman and to die, unsexed, in the gutter; or for creature-comforts and a good name to sell herself, soul and body, into life-long bondage ...

In 1896 the papers were combined and published under the title *Love's Coming of Age*, from which the above statement is taken.[4]

The first, most important pamphlet, *Sex-Love and Its Place in a Free Society*, opened the case for 'the enfranchisement of the body', first proclaimed twenty years earlier in *Towards Democracy*. In it, he tackled head-on the issue of repressed sexuality; arguing that the restraints placed on the natural expression of the sex instinct were highly damaging to the development of the individual. But there was no common acceptance of this need, for *either* sex, especially for women. This enforced celibacy, he argued, would in the social life of the future be seen as 'almost as grievous as that of prostitution...'[5] This was a dangerous challenge to the Victorian belief that the single purpose of sexual relations was procreation. For many, in endorsing female sexual pleasure, Carpenter posed a greater danger as an instigator of sexual anarchy, than as a defender of homosexuality.

Although the strength of his support for women was made abundantly clear in the pamphlets, it is surprising that, over the years, he has not found favour with a number of feminist writers. Recognition of his role has been largely confined to his call for women's economic liberation. For one contemporary feminist, Carpenter's work does not even merit a mention, although *Love's Coming of Age* is listed in the bibliography.[6] In particular, feminists have objected to the biological *essentialism* underlying Carpenter's writing on women, choosing to ignore the fact that it was then the prevailing scientific orthodoxy. With biology already giving way to genetics, it was inevitable that inherent female characteristics, not those produced by social ascription and conditioning, should be the bedrock of late-nineteenth-century thinking about gender. At the time, it was accepted that each sex possessed fixed biological characteristics, which controlled physiological drives and emotional responses. Ellis's *Man and Woman*, published at the same time as Carpenter's pamphlets, was an extensive study of 'secondary sexual differences' relevant to the issues surrounding gender. [7]

It was the nascent sciences of embryology and neurology that informed late-nineteenth-century thinking about gender, not gender *formation* through social conditioning. Carpenter accepted that there were biologically-determined differences, physiological, psychological and cognitive, between the sexes, which made them not equal but complementary. But, if he held the then conventional view of the biological basis of gender, of fixed female characteristics, this never limited his vision of women's potential. He rejected the idea that 'the good woman' was no more than a child-bearer, a charge made by another feminist writer, who considered it to be 'the source of the anti-feminist thread running through the polemical homosexual literature of the period'.[8] Whilst child-bearing was a woman's 'most perfect work', there was a greater womanhood to be achieved, one which, as Schreiner argued, required 'her complete freedom as to the disposal of her sex'.[9]

More damaging for Carpenter, is the claim that his separation of sex from the function of procreation was a clever ploy to justify a homosexual erotic life. The defence of same-sex love was the hidden agenda, enabling him to exonerate the homosexual 'from the charge of licentiousness'. The claim is that he used the women's cause for his own selfish purposes.[10] However, there is little to support the argument that it was his intended defence of homosexuality that 'inspired his analysis of heterosexual relations rather than the reverse'.[11] He is also criticised for lacking an understanding of the tensions between women's reproductive function and their sexual lives. He was 'disinclined to give reproduction any weight at all'.[12]

In another early assessment, Sheila Rowbotham regretted that, while he listened to the sex-related troubles of his educated, articulate middle-class women friends, he absorbed little on the problems of being a working-class woman, notably on issues of fertility, pregnancy and motherhood. Although he was in a position to understand working-class women's experiences, he didn't tap into it. But that these women would have been reluctant to discuss such matters, even with their own husbands let alone with Carpenter, is not considered. And the fact that he only wrote in passing about his relationships with the wives of artisans, is not a sufficient ground for claiming that he 'wrote about women's oppression from the outside'. He spent years observing life, both in the middle-class villa, where the woman of the house 'sits in state and has her tea', *and* the cottage, where 'the men take their ease and are served by the woman'. He knew that many working-class women, if leading lives of 'more honesty and reality' than the 'lady', were steeped in drudgery, and at worst in conditions of 'abject slavery': [13]

> What a sight, in any of our great towns, to enter into the cottages or tenements ... to find in each one a working wife struggling alone in semi-darkness and seclusion with the toils of an entire separate household ... wearied and worried, debilitated with confinement and want of fresh air, and low spirited for want of change and society.[14]

He was interacting daily with the two working-class women who, in succession, provided for his domestic comfort at Millthorpe; arrangements that he maintained for several years. The picture of a Carpenter remaining aloof, unable to overcome the divisions of class and sex, is not plausible. Living among the wives of artisans and farm labourers gave him a much greater understanding of the untapped qualities of working-class women than most men of his status. In contrast to the artificial, controlled and wasted life of the 'lady' he saw one kind of female ideal in the countrywomen, 'who manage cattle well, and gardens, and understand the breeding of sheep'.[15]

> The modern woman sees plainly enough that no decent advance for her sex is possible until this whole question (of her status) is fairly faced. – involving, as of course it will do, a life very different from her present one, far more in the open air, with real bodily exercise and development, some amount of regular manual work, a knowledge of the laws of health and physiology, an altogether wider mental outlook, and greater

self-reliance and nature-hardihood. But when once these things are granted, she sees that she will no longer be the serf, but the equal, the mate and the comrade of Man.[16]

A further criticism of his writing on women is that he was tainted by a misogyny stemming from his 'aesthetic' preference for the male body. He never denied how he felt towards a woman as an erotic object, which was no different from his lesbian friend Kate Salt's reaction to the male body; her 'instinctive repulsion for any physical intimacy with the other sex'.[17] Others have associated him with homosexual men of the 1890s who were supposedly intent upon preserving male dominance and male separatism, in the belief that they had more in common with heterosexual men. If homosexual 'identity-formation' depended strongly on such misogyny, then homosexual men 'could not be dependable allies'.[18] Carpenter was well aware that there were misogynistic homosexual men, typically men who had little or no contact with women, and who regarded relationships between men as more spiritual and purer than heterosexual relationships:

> That men of this kind despise women is not an uncommon belief, but is hardly justified. Though naturally not inclined to 'fall in love' such men are by their nature drawn rather nearer to women, and it would seem that they often feel a singular appreciation and understanding of the emotional needs and destinies of the other sex, leading in many cases to a genuine though what is called 'Platonic Friendship' ... They are not seldom the faithfulest of friends, the truest allies and most convinced defenders of women.[19]

There is little doubt that this was Schreiner's view of Carpenter. If he had been at all misogynistic, the highly sensitive Olive would never have opened herself to him. Almost from the beginning of their friendship he was her 'beautiful boy', her 'darling', her 'big brother'. She would tell him: 'Edward, I love you so dear, you have entered right into my heart'.[20] A special bond had been forged between them. Schreiner was the 'new woman' in search of the 'new man', and it was the homosexual Carpenter who may have come closest to this ideal; closer than either of the progressive intellectuals, Havelock Ellis and Karl Pearson, with whom she had become emotionally entangled when in England.

In one of her last letters before returning to the Cape Province, she told him: 'I have been passing through much darkness and when I have looked around the world for a ray of light I have found you. Go on your path Edward, my beautiful brother. Some far-off day to come it will be seen what a light you were, how far before your time'.[21].

10

From Pathology to Biology

The development of forensic psychiatry in Europe in the mid-1850s created a new interest in the causes of deviant sexuality. The focus moved from a generalised view that such behaviour was the result of sexual excess or moral depravity to the clinical examination of real cases. As medical and legal journals began to fill with studies of inmates of prisons and mental asylums, a consensus emerged that such sexual behaviour pointed to a degenerative disorder. Consequently, gay men now faced a double struggle: against the criminalisation of homosexual acts and its pathologisation. But, in 1864, Karl Heinrich Ulrichs, an obscure Hanoverian jurist, challenged this consensus and transformed the debate on the nature of homosexuality. Thirty years later, his ideas would become a controversial part of Carpenter's own characterisation of the homosexual.

Under the pseudonym Numa Numantius, Ulrichs published the first of a series of booklets on the *Riddle of Love between Men*,[1] which moved the discussion of homosexuality from forensic psychiatry to biology. Ulrichs claimed that homosexual desire was the result of an abnormal development of the embryo, which influenced the function of the psyche in determining the direction of the sex-drive. The possibility that there were males who differed from heterosexuals in their psychic natures was scientifically ground-breaking. For the first time, a class of persons could be identified and named. Before this bold idea, only sexual acts had been recognised, not persons with definable sexual natures.

Ulrichs could not explain why or how this occurred but a new phase in the understanding of homosexuality had been opened up, challenging the morbidity argument and offering a credible scientific explanation. This judgement has lasted.[2] The new focus on the phenomenon as an embryological abnormality, rather than a pathological condition, was to prove a step-change in the understanding of homosexuality. Today, the link between biology and sexual orientation is a fertile ground for research, with the early uterine environment identified as one possible factor, while other studies point to the role of pre-natal hormonal exposure.

Importantly, Ulrichs was also the first to pose a fundamental moral question: whether any society had the right to punish individuals who, as he believed, came into the world with homosexual instincts? Homosexuals had a right to satisfy their sex-drive, and its expression between consenting adults should only be open to legal sanction if it involved the seduction of minors, was achieved by force or threat, or offended public decency:

> Every living being in creation is justified by the right of nature to fulfil the demands of the natural sex drive, because they are based on natural law and necessity of nature, and because the drive itself is implanted by nature. No living being can be required to suppress this drive for life as a duty.[3]
>
> We are not eunuchs. Nature gave us, like you, a sexual drive,

which needs to be gratified. Also, we have taken no vows of chastity … We too have a right to enjoy the pleasures of love; we too, have the right to satisfy our sexual drives; we too have the right to do this in the manner that is natural for us, not in any other way.[4]

With a lawyer's skill, Ulrichs dissected those parts of Hanover's penal code controlling sexual behaviour; exposing the irrational and often illogical treatment of the homosexual, when compared with the heterosexual. He challenged legislators and jurists to question the assumptions about human sexuality that determined their law-making and judicial decisions:

> The Urning, [Ulrichs coined this term for the male homosexual] is also a citizen. He too, has civil rights; and according to these rights, the state has certain duties to fulfil as well. The state does not have the right to act on whimsy or for the sheer love of persecution. The state is not authorised, as in the past, to treat Urnings as outside the pale of the law.[5]

In his eleventh booklet, *Araxes*, he penned the first comprehensive, strikingly modern, statement of homosexual rights, opening with the claim:

> The Urning too is a person. He too, therefore has inalienable rights. His sexual orientation is a right established by nature. Legislators have no right to veto nature; no right to persecute nature in the course of its work; no right to torture living creatures who are subject to those drives nature gave them.[6]

Ulrichs's theory of the origin of the homosexual drive separated sex physiology from sex psychology, thus challenging the assumption that the physiology of the individual determined sexual feelings. If sexually inverted males with normal genitalia were not physically attracted to women, physiology could not be the determinant of sexual orientation. The sexual drive had to be controlled by the psyche. This led him to conclude that such individuals, in so far as the *sexual drive* was concerned, possessed female psyches. A female 'sex-love' could reside in a male body, and likewise, a male sex-love in a female body. Individuals with normal male sexual organs, but a sexual drive towards the same sex, were neither fully men nor fully women, leading him to assert that the sexually inverted constituted a third sex, *das dratted geschlecht*. And it followed that there had to be a fourth sex made up of women who possessed a normal female sexual anatomy but a male sex-drive. In both cases, there was a discordance between body and mind stemming from the abnormal development of the embryo. This directly challenged the dimorphic model of gender: the assumption that all individuals were naturally male or female. In confronting dimorphism, Ulrichs could claim to have put forward 'the first scientific theory of homosexuality'.[7] Subsequent researchers, mainly physicians, made reference to it, even though the consensus remained that homosexuality was a neuropathic or psychopathic condition.

The idea of homosexuals as a third sex did not seem to be an entailment of Ulrichs's initial hypothesis, and when it was underpinned by *feminisation* it became highly controversial. It suggested that all male homosexuals experienced a gender identity that was inconsistent with their physiological sex. But Ulrichs took it as axiomatic that sexual love of a man for a man must be a feminine drive. Gender inversion was psychological, but simply arguing that the unobservable psychologically determined sex-drive was feminine, would hardly convince. Initially, he argued that all male homosexuals could be identified by manifest female characteristics and gender non-conformity in childhood. He drew on his own childhood, focussing on what he considered to be his feminine nature: his desire to be dressed as a girl and his partiality for girlish activities and a girl's playthings. This feminine element in his nature, he believed, was a consequence of his sexual love-drive. The body of the homosexual, he claimed, also displayed feminine traits, with some specifically male features, body shape, voice, beard, deportment, being absent. But these arguments began to unravel when men who were sexually inverted did not report such feminine behaviour in childhood, and regarded their bodies and behaviours as masculine.

Those who knew Ulrichs well did not regard him as feminine. He was, for his times, seen as conventionally gendered. But he was acquainted with homosexuals who called themselves sisters and gave themselves female names, and this reinforced his view. And the idea of the feminisation of homosexuals had historical credence in the subculture of 'mollies', where feminine dress, the assumption of female roles in homosexual relationships and mock marriages were common. But nothing in these behaviours necessarily denoted gender inversion.[8]

Notwithstanding the historical importance of Ulrichs's claims, his central idea of a unique homosexual *persona* was contradicted by the emerging evidence of homosexual diversity. With greater knowledge of the lives of homosexuals, and influenced by individuals who had read his monographs and written to him, he realised that there were men who loved women and men alike; that there were men who loved other men tenderly and sentimentally but desired women sexually. And it was abundantly clear that there were individuals who were homosexual but who possessed all the physical and many of the intellectual and emotional characteristics of men who were not. On the other hand, there were clearly many men who possessed the feminine characteristics described by Ulrichs who were not feminine in the *psychic* sense, because they were not attracted sexually to men.

The identification of supposedly feminine traits or characteristics in sexually inverted men and, on the other hand, masculine traits in sexually inverted women, would not seem necessary to support Ulrichs's key biological explanation for the direction of the sexual instinct. If feminine traits were not necessarily markers of sexual inversion, the feminisation of the homosexual in the public mind was given credence by the third sex theorising that Ulrichs set in train.

Ulrichs went on to develop a classification of homosexual types, in the form of a continuum between the modern polarities of 'gay' and 'straight'. A parallel continuum was also constructed for female sexual orientation. In doing so, he rendered his initial third-sex theory untenable, and the complete feminine personality that he had earlier insisted always marked out the homosexual could no longer hold. But the two most influential followers of Ulrichs, in Germany Magnus Hirschfeld, and, as we shall see, in England Carpenter, retained, against considerable opposition, the idea of a feminised homosexual.

11

—

A Fateful Collaboration

When, in 1890, Havelock Ellis published his first book, *The New Spirit*,[1] in which he sought to capture the ethos of his times expressed in the work of leading writers of the day, he sent a copy to the English literary critic John Addington Symonds. Symonds was quick to note that the book included a chapter on Walt Whitman and he took the opportunity to quiz Ellis on the homoerotic strain in the poet's *Leaves of Grass*: '[Is] he willing to accept, condone or ignore the physical aspects of the passion', he asked.[2] In a passage seized upon by prurient critics, Ellis had written that Whitman 'finds the roots of the most universal love in the intimate and physical love of comrades and lovers'. He made reference to one of the most homoerotic of Whitman's poems and posed the question: 'Why should the sweetening breath of science be guarded from this spot'?[3]

It was only weeks after Carpenter's discovery of Whitman's poetry that Symonds had also come across Rossetti's collection. He would never meet the poet but wrote a month before Whitman's death: 'Brought up in the purple of aristocratic school and university, provided with more money than is good for a young man … I might have been a mere English gentleman, had not I read *Leaves of Grass* in time'.[4] When Rossetti sent him a piece of Whitman's hand-writing he told a friend: 'I wd [*sic*] as soon have this as that of Shakespeare or Plato or Dante'.[5]

Symonds had written and privately circulated two monographs on homosexuality. The first, A *Problem in Greek Ethics* (1887), was an examination of the practice of paederastia in ancient Greece. He wanted to offer a different perspective from the one usually adopted by writers on homosexuality. The neglect of cultural history in the examination of the subject troubled him deeply, and he set out to show that, within the refined civilisations of a small number of Greek city states, homosexual relationships between aristocratic youths and men had been recognised and utilised for the benefit of the individual and society. He marshalled a wide range of historical and literary material to illustrate the forms that it had taken, its relationship to Greek aesthetic values and, importantly, the ethical attitude of the Greeks towards it. He hoped that by writing about what was an aspect of one of the most brilliant periods of human history, and a relationship that some Greeks thought to be superior to heterosexual love, he might mitigate Victorian hostility.

The second, *A Problem in Modern Ethics* (1891), was a direct outcome of the passing of the 1885 Criminal Law Amendment Act. Symonds wrote it to contest this legislation, by advancing a case for the decriminalisation of homosexual acts between consenting adults that took place in private. It was a political manifesto; the first to focus on the predicament of the homosexual in England. Although it was written to help to establish a case for the partial decriminalisation of homosexuality, Symonds had a broader objective: to engage critically with current ideas on the nature of homosexuality, and for the monograph to be received, not as a polemic, but as a well-researched contribution to the subject.

He was considering combining the two monographs in a book and asked Ellis if he would take it for a new series on contemporary science that he was then editing. When Ellis prevaricated, considering homosexuality a subject too risky for his series, Symonds, out of the blue, suggested that they might jointly author a book, if not for the series. He gave no reason for his change of mind but he must have concluded that his severe criticism of the views of continental physicians and psychologists in the *Modern Problem* could easily be set aside as those of a known homosexual, and also a layman. He told Carpenter, who he had now come to know through their mutual admiration of Whitman: 'I need somebody of medical importance to collaborate with. Alone I could make but little effect – the effect of an eccentric'.[6]

His approach was timely, as unbeknown to him Ellis was preparing to make the study of human sexuality his life's work. But of much more significance, he was equally unaware that, at this very time, Ellis was facing a personal crisis, after discovering that Edith Lees, the woman who he had married only six months earlier, was attracted to women. This was the decisive factor in Ellis's decision to collaborate with Symonds on the writing of what would become *Sexual Inversion*, the book for which he is now best known. It triggered a need in Ellis to explore a sexuality that challenged his masculinity and blighted his marriage. If he had not agreed to collaborate, this ground-breaking book would never have been written. Acutely aware of Victorian attitudes towards homosexuality, he knew that rather than collaborating on a book on the subject he should have passed it over as a distasteful topic on which it was not wise to enlarge. Later, he acknowledged that writing it had been a mistake, and claimed that it had never been his intention to launch his career as a sexual theorist with such a topic. But his decision to collaborate was critical because it propelled Symonds, and then Carpenter, into the field of sexual politics.

Having agreed to work on a book with Symonds, Ellis told Carpenter: 'We want to obtain sympathetic recognition for sexual inversion [homosexuality] as a psychic abnormality which may be regarded as the highest ideal, & to clear away many vulgar errors – preparing the way, if possible, for a change in the law. Nothing of the kind has yet been published, at least in England, & I cannot help feeling that the book will do much good'.[7]

Carpenter was keen to help and offered to provide notes on his own observations and experience. At the time, he was writing his women-related pamphlets, but the notes may have been preparation for the *Homogenic Love* pamphlet that was to follow. He also agreed to help with obtaining autobiographical accounts from other homosexual men. Symonds drew up a questionnaire and Carpenter used it among his friends and was able to provide a number of sexual histories, including his own.

In a flurry of letters, Ellis and Symonds exchanged ideas on what should be in the book, especially the integration of parts of Symonds's monographs; how it should be structured; the division of labour between them and how to get more histories of the sexual lives of homosexual men. Then, in April 1893, before they could even meet, Symonds died.[8]

Carpenter was saddened, and also dismayed, by Symonds's death. Believing that such a book was sorely needed in England, he did not want the project to collapse. He urged Ellis to press on and became his principal point of reference on all matters to do with homosexuality. Being much more on top of the current literature than Ellis, he advised him on the works that he should read; offered his own careful analyses and evaluations of these; provided him with more case histories; read, at Ellis's invitation, his drafts; and suggested changes. This gave him an important, not fully recognised, role in the book's gestation and progression. It is clear from their written exchanges that Ellis benefited greatly from his guidance and advice, consolidated by their face-to-face meetings in the British Museum when Carpenter was in London, but there is no indication in their papers or letters that Carpenter might have replaced Symonds as Ellis's collaborator.

12

——

Darkening Clouds

Oscar Wilde's conviction for gross indecency, in April 1895, cast a deep shadow over Carpenter's resolve to state the case for the homosexual. But even without this scandal, the time was hardly opportune for such an undertaking. In 1889, there had been a widely publicised scandal surrounding a male brothel in Cleveland Street, off Tottenham Court Road in the West End of London. During an investigation into a theft at the Central Telegraph Office a delivery boy was found in possession of a large sum of money. When questioned, he confessed that he had been given it for 'going to bed with gentlemen'. Soon other boys were implicated and began naming prominent persons as clients of the brothel. As well as members of Parliament, Lord Arthur Somerset, a superintendent of the Royal stables, was implicated, and it was hinted that Prince Eddy, the son of the Prince of Wales, was also a visitor. The Earl of Euston and Lord Arthur Clifton were also named and very quickly it developed into 'the most elusive and mysterious affair of Queen Victoria's reign'.[1]

Public alarm, stirred up by lurid newspaper accounts of the scandal, was not the only obstacle Carpenter faced. Coded, sometimes even explicit, homoerotic literature was being openly published, with an efflorescence of poetry and prose associated with the Uranian school of poets. It was a close-knit group of individuals who shared an idealisation of pre-pubescent or adolescent boys, and whose verse and prose, full of literary artifice, was a cover for either sexless devotion or homosexual passion: 'They wrote to sublimate their love, not to display their talents; for each other's entertainment, not for the public ear. If they could fool the world by supressing the sex of their beloved and so earn a few pennies from publishing their verse, they did so'.[2]

In 1892, John Gambril Nicholson published *Love in Earnest*, a collection of sonnets, ballads and lyrics, in which the sex of the love object was not disclosed, but the heavily paederastic collection was a word play on the Christian name of a boy at a school where Nicholson was an assistant master. Other writers or artists of the day who were fixated on young boys or youths included William Johnson Corry, Ernest Dowson, Charles Masson Fox, and Charles Keynes-Jackson, who wrote a sonnet on a picture of Falmouth fisher-boys painted by boy-lover Henry Scott Tuke. Frederick Rolfe (Baron Corvo) sent Fox photographs of naked Italian youths, together with long graphic descriptions of sex with compliant boys picked up in the slums of Venice.

The following year, a five guinea, highly explicit, erotic novel of homosexual love, *Teleny or The Reverse of the Medal* appeared.[3] It carried no author's name, but Wilde was immediately thought to have had some part in its composition. In 1894, a new literary periodical, *The Yellow Book*,[4] was launched, with a distinctive binding and decoration by Aubrey Beardsley, whose androgynous illustrations were denounced by the prominent art critic Harry Quilter as perverted for depicting manhood and womanhood mingled together 'in a monstrous sexless amalgam'.[5] The periodical was viewed with suspicion as the new trumpet-piece of the 'Decadents', a group of writers who occupied a transitional period between romanticism and modernism. It originated in France, and in England it was chiefly applied to those associated with *The Yellow Book*. Its opening editorial proclaimed that it would 'have the courage of its modernness, and not tremble at the frown of Mrs Grundy'. During its three years of life, discreetly homosexual individuals, including Henry James and Edmund Gosse, contributed, but it projected an air of respectability by drawing in others, such as Arnold Bennett and W. B. Yeats. In the same year, a scandalising novel, *The Green Carnation*, was published anonymously in London. On the opening night of Oscar Wilde's first society comedy, *Lady Windermere's Fan*, a dozen young men had sported a carnation dyed green, already a symbol of homosexuality in Paris. It was well-known in homosexual circles that the author of the novel was Robert Hitchens, a friend of Lord Alfred Douglas, Oscar Wilde's lover, and on the fringes of the Wilde circle. Its principal character was seen as a thinly disguised portrait of Wilde, which satirised him 'just within the laws of libel'.[6] Its depiction of a network of men corrupting boys gave it the appearance of a manifesto for sodomites.

The novel appeared when a growing storm of scandal was beginning to swirl around Wilde and Douglas. Wilde was incensed enough to write to the *Pall Mall Gazette*, 'to contradict, in the most emphatic manner' the suggestion that he was the author.[7] He could not bear to think that such a mediocre piece of literature might be attributed to him. Vanity blinded him to the obvious danger of drawing attention to himself, ensuring that his name became more widely associated with the book.

Also in 1894, John Francis Bloxam, an Oxford undergraduate, produced a magazine, *The Chameleon*,[8] in which the subterranean theme was boy-love. The very first issue included a scandalising paederastic story, *The Priest and the Acolyte*, written by Bloxam. It also carried a collection of epigrams by Wilde, *Phrases and*

Philosophies for the Use of the Young. This was cited during the libel action brought by Wilde against the Marquess of Queensberry, as evidence of Wilde's association with a publication 'calculated to subvert morality and to encourage unnatural vice'. After Wilde withdrew his libel action against Queensberry, in April 1895 he faced two trials for 'gross indecency' with rent boys, under the 1885 Criminal Law Amendment Act. Wilde had also contributed to *The Spirit Lamp*, another Oxford undergraduate periodical, of which a number of issues were edited by Douglas. It appealed 'to all who are interested in modern life and the new culture'. *The Artist and Journal of Home Culture*, edited by the paederast Kains-Jackson, was a similarly innocuous-sounding publication that carried a good deal of homoerotic poetry and fiction.

After Wilde's conviction, three articles appeared in a single issue of the influential *Contemporary Review*. Sir Clifford Allbutt, in *Nervous Diseases and Modern Life*, warned that it was necessary to guard against 'the encroachment of peoples of lower standards and lower ethical capacities upon the seats of nations'; J. A. Noble exposed *The Fiction of Sexuality*, and Harry Quilter attacked *The Gospel of Intensity*.[9]

13

Born Lovers of
Their Own Sex

If the content of the three women-related pamphlets was provocative, they had not attracted the attention of the censor. In January 1895, although dated 1894, he released a further pamphlet, with the title *Homogenic Love and its Place in a Free Society*.[1] To publish an unequivocal defence of homosexuality at such a time was a dangerous undertaking and required exceptional literary skills: 'No word or hint of impropriety ever sullied his pages … The mystery, perhaps, lay in his tact, his charm and his cunning use of words'.[2]

His earlier pamphlets were aimed at freeing women from the bondage of the Victorian hearth and marriage bed. He now turned to attack the harsh legal and social edicts against same-sex love. His modernity was startling. He did not ask simply for tolerance for such a love, a plea that would become a central concern of sexual liberationists in the following century. He sought public recognition of the homosexual orientation as a natural, stable variant of human sexuality. As such, the pamphlet was, he later recalled, 'among the first attempts in this country to deal at all publicly' with the issue of homosexuality, and the first declaration by an Englishman that linked sexual emancipation to social transformation.[3]

Running to over fifty pages, it was couched in everyday language and was aimed at the educated reader, not the medical and legal professions. But, as the subject was surrounded by 'anathemas and execrations', he was well aware that the pamphlet would almost certainly be deemed obscene if it came to the attention of the authorities. It was not sold but 'sent round pretty freely to those who I thought would be interested in the subject or able to contribute views or information upon it'.[4] The title of the pamphlet demonstrated his characteristic shrewdness, by introducing a new word, *homogenic*, which was derived entirely from the Greek, and was therefore linguistically purer than homosexual. His intention was to remove undue stress on the physical side of this love, and for the same reason, he would occasionally use the noun *homophile*. The pamphlet opened with a short historical survey of homosexual persons found in widely differing cultures in which they had a distinctive social function. History, literature, art and modern science, all revealed that the homogenic passion was 'capable of splendid developments, well worthy of respectful and thoughtful consideration'. This was tactical: to give the reader 'some idea of the place and position in the world of (this) particular sentiment'.[5]

The principal works on homosexuality at this time were continental; German, French and Italian. The most significant of these was Richard Krafft-Ebing's *Psychopathia Sexualis*, which appeared in an English translation in 1892. He had developed the 'psychiatric case-history' and a taxonomy of sexual-types based upon the detailed analysis of a large number of histories. Most were of lower-class individuals found in the public asylums and clinics where Krafft-Ebing practised as a medical superintendent. He also took private patients, which brought him into contact with a different class of homosexual. Many were educated individuals from the higher ranks of society who, after reading *Psychopathia Sexualis*, wrote to him with accounts of their sexual histories. These autobiographical narratives formed an indispensable component in the fashioning of sexual categories and the classification of sexual behaviour. For the first time, in any significant numbers, homosexuals spoke for themselves, and these self-analyses provided material for new psychiatric insights. If, as is often claimed, the 'homosexual' was a late-nineteenth-century social construction, then self-construction by such individuals was an essential element in the process. Addressed principally to physicians and lawyers, *Psychopathia Sexualis* treated male homosexual behaviour as an abnormal deviation from procreative sexual intercourse; the male sexual norm expressed by the noun 'heterosexual', which had been coined in Germany in 1869 by Karl-Maria Kertbeny.

Carpenter utilised Krafft-Ebing's findings to support his claim that the homosexual orientation was an *innate* biologically-determined drive:

> It seems a strange oversight that science, to date, has taken little interest in this matter – a desire for corporeal intimacy of some kind between persons of the same sex existing in such force and so widely it would seem almost certain that there must be some physiological basis for the desire. Until we know more than we do at present as to what the basis may be, we are necessarily unable to understand the desire itself as well as we might wish.[6]

Without an understanding of the psychology of love, the inverted sex-feeling could no more be explained than could the normal impulse. The critical question then became, not whether the instinct was capable of 'morbid and extravagant manifestation', but whether it was capable of 'a healthy and sane expression.'[7]

The medico-scientific investigators, whose field of research was usually in great modern cities, were bound to meet with some cases that were of a morbid character and it was no wonder that the idea of disease coloured their conclusions. But Krafft-Ebing's findings had begun to dispel the view that the passion was always associated with 'distinct disease, either physical or mental'.[8] Carpenter foresaw a time when such terms describing the general sentiment of love towards a person of the same sex would finally be abandoned.

It was important to insist that individuals who were homosexual did not differ from heterosexual men in any identifiable physical or mental particular, although he believed that there was a 'general tendency' towards 'femininity of type' in the male homosexual, and of masculinity in the female (discussed in chapter eighteen). There was 'no congenital malformation, no distinct disease of body or mind'.[9] The attraction, both mentally and physically, to one of the same sex was 'in a vast number of cases quite instinctive, twined in the very roots of individual life and practically ineradicable'.[10] So deeply was it fixed in a person's mental and emotional life, that such an individual had difficulty in imagining himself being otherwise: '[T]o him at least the homogenic love appears healthy and natural, and indeed necessary to the concretation [*sic*] of his individuality'.[11] Emphasising the instinctive, congenital characteristic of homosexuality was critical in distinguishing 'born lovers of their own sex' from persons who, out of curiosity, excessive sexual arousal, or from a lack of opportunities for heterosexual intercourse, adopted homosexual practices.

Whatever a person's sexual orientation, all individuals had a need to love and to be loved. As Ulrichs had argued, individuals for whom such ties could only be found with a person of the same sex should not be denied the fulfilment of this need. Carpenter recognised that to represent same-sex attachments as purely spiritual in nature would be disingenuous, and acknowledged that some degree of physical intimacy was as much a necessity, and a condition of healthy life, as it was for the heterosexual. But, it is hardly surprising that he stressed that there was a 'tendency' for this love to express itself more through the emotions, going as far as to suggest that in a large number of cases it was 'not distinctly sexual at all, though it may be said to be physical in the sense of embrace and endearment'.[12] Certainly, if bodily intimacy or endearment was denied, it would 'bar any real sense of repose and affiance, and make the relation restless, vague, tentative and unsatisfied'.[13] It was not the case that 'the lower or more physical manifestations of love should be killed out in order to force the growth of the more spiritual and enduring forms.' The natural desire for physical intimacies could never be eliminated, while 'intimacies founded on intellectual and moral affinities alone are seldom very deep and lasting. If the physical basis 'in any form is quite absent, the acquaintanceship is liable to die away'.[14]

Having argued that a healthy homosexual love could not be without its physical side, he had to deal with the difficult question of what *form* of intimacy was 'fitting and natural'. He could not avoid tackling head-on the association of physical intimacy between males with one form of sensuality only, sodomy. It was the most rigidly proscribed and denounced of all male sexual practices, and the Latinate term *'venus aversa, contra naturum'* was often used to avoid naming it. During the Wilde trials, sodomy will become fixed in the public mind as the defining act of the male homosexual, for no other sexual act will be named. It was, therefore, essential to insist that any physical intimacy between two persons of the same sex should not be, 'set down as a sexual act of the crudest and grossest kind'.[15]

There was a further significant distinction to be made. Homosexuality should not be confused with paedophilia; with a sexual desire for boys, thereby casting the homosexual as a corrupter of the innocent. Whilst never denying the existence of the paedophile, Carpenter aimed to sever this connection by presenting the homosexual drive as a desire for adult sexual partners. His defence of a homosexuality that was exclusively *androphilic*, not in the least concerned with boys, was timely. Even before Wilde, as we have seen, the link between homosexuality and paedophilia was invariably made.

As the title of the pamphlet indicated, his defence of the homosexual temperament goes beyond a plea for its recognition and acceptance as part of human sexuality. He takes forward the cultural arguments that had been so important for Symonds, extolling the moral value and social worth of such individuals. Some thirty pages of Ellis's *Sexual Inversion*, provided by Symonds, will be devoted to accounts of homosexual individuals of exceptional intellectual and artistic abilities. Freed from the responsibilities and impedimenta of family life, such individuals could 'supply the force and liberate the energies required for social and mental activities of the most necessary kind'. It was doubtful whether, 'the higher heroic and spiritual life' of a nation was possible without the sanctioning of the homosexual attachment. Just as the ordinary sex-love had a special function in the propagation of the race, 'so the other love should have its special function in social and heroic work, and in the generation – not of bodily children – but of those children of the mind, the philosophical conceptions and ideals which transform our lives and those of society'.[16] The homogenic attachment had 'the deepest relations to general politics'; a role in 'the life-long building up of new forms of society, new orders of thought, and new institutions of human solidarity'.[17]

The advance of women, also required a fuller recognition of the place of the homogenic sentiment in their emotional and sexual lives:

It is noticeable, too, in the deepest relation to politics, that the movement among women towards their own liberation and emancipation which is taking place all over the civilised

121

world has been accompanied by a marked development of the homogenic passion among the female sex ... such comrade-alliances – and of a quite passionate kind – are becoming increasingly common, and especially perhaps among the more cultured classes of women, who are working out the great cause of their sex's liberation.[18]

The pamphlet concluded with a call for the ending of the prosecution, under the 1885 Criminal Law Amendment Act, of homosexual acts between consenting adults that took place in private. In the face of growing evidence that the homosexual orientation was an innate drive, it was unjust to legislate against a natural inclination:

> If the dedication of love were a matter of mere choice or whim, it still would not be the business of the State to compel that choice but since no amount of compulsion can ever change the homogenic instinct in a person, where it is innate, the State in trying to effect such a change is only kicking vainly against the pricks of its own advantage, and trying, in view perhaps of the conduct of a licentious few, to cripple and damage a respectable and valuable class of its own citizens.[19]

Law could not control the expression of feeling, and in employing the clumsy bludgeon of the statute book to criminalise homosexual acts between consenting adults in private, the government was acting as a moral censor, adjudicating upon conduct that was properly a personal choice. This was not the law's province, and even were it, such a law could not possibly be enforced. And because it did not require such private acts to be witnessed, it opened, wider than before, the door to the blackmailer:

> That the homosexual passion may be improperly indulged in, that it may lead, like the heterosexual, to public abuses of liberty

and decency we of course do not deny; but, as in the case of persons of opposite sex, the law limits itself on the whole to the maintenance of public order, the protection of the weak from violence and insult, and of the young from their inexperience: so it should be here.[20]

The quality of the pamphlet was recognised by Ellis, who sent a copy to Horatio Brown, Symonds's literary executor. Writing from Venice, Brown was fulsome in his praise for Carpenter's special talents:

> I should like to tell you with what admiration, sympathy & enthusiasm I have read it. It is in this cool, quiet, convincing, scientific way that I think this difficult & at present obscure problem should be brought to the notice of an ignorant and hostile society. At present I am rather afraid of the effect upon the world if the polemic is confined to the region of belles lettres. I ought to say it more simply; I mean that I think we want a cool, unimpassioned statement of the situation & that Doctors & Lawyers must be induced to take off their spectacles and look.[21]

Brown asked for copies: 'I want to send it to many unconvinced – also to some who need no convincing but who would be drawn towards the writer of this calm statement of an observed case'.[22] However, not all of Carpenter's homosexual friends were as enthusiastic as Brown. Goldsworthy Lowes Dickinson ruminated: 'I suppose it is all in order, though I have a kind of feeling that these things are better left unsaid. Perhaps it is just because science has a way of treating these things as phenomena merely, that I think they should not be printed'.[23] But he clearly admired Carpenter for his bravery in writing the pamphlet: 'How it is that public opinion hasn't managed to get him into prison and murder him, is a mystery to me. We must be thankful for small mercies.[24]

The pamphlet was reviewed in *Humanity*, the journal of the Humanitarian League, edited by Carpenter's friend Henry Salt. His first three pamphlets had dealt with 'the most difficult and delicate questions' and deserved to be even more widely known. But it was right that the homogenic love pamphlet was privately circulated, 'since anything which may be said on the subject is likely to be misunderstood at the present time', clearly a reference to the Wilde trials. The reviewer regretted that, 'through dread of public opinion', English scientific men were silent on the subject.[25] Ellis's book, *Sexual Inversion*, had yet to see the light of day.

14

A Literary Inquisition

Encouraged by the success of the women-related pamphlets, he put them together, added new material, and got a book ready. The rigidity of public opinion towards sexual matters, 'the absolute determination of people to *misunderstand* if they possibly could'[1] meant that nearly every chapter was rewritten four or five times over before he was satisfied with it. The book was to be called *The Sexes in a Free Society*.

He sounded out the publisher Fisher Unwin, whose titles now included the third edition of *Towards Democracy*. The quite progressive Unwin agreed to publish the book at his own expense, but only a few weeks later, as Carpenter was fond of saying, the bottom dropped out of his little bucket. On 26 April 1895, a libel action, for defamation, brought by Oscar Wilde against the Marquess of Queensberry, was withdrawn after Wilde's counsel learned of the witnesses Queensberry intended to call: young men who had prostituted themselves with Wilde. Queensberry was determined that Wilde should face a criminal trial and his solicitor sent a copy of the youths' incriminating statements to the Director of Public Prosecutions.

A warrant for Wilde's arrest, for 'committing acts of gross indecency with other male persons', was granted by Sir John Bridge at Bow Street Magistrates Court. According to some accounts, Bridge, possibly to avoid another sensational trial in which the sexual peccadilloes of persons in high places might well have been revealed, dated the warrant for a quarter of an hour after the departure of the last continental boat-train from Dover. It gave Wilde time to flee, but he ignored his friends' entreaties and retired to the Cadogan Hotel, a stone's throw from his Knightsbridge home, where he waited with friends, fortified by copious alcohol and cigarettes.

Wilde's arrest set alarm bells ringing in gay circles. For some, prudence was the order of the day. Frank Harris, Wilde's erstwhile friend and biographer, described, if a little imaginatively, its effect on those who feared that the trial would lay bare London's homosexual underworld and draw others into the net closing around Wilde:

> Every train to Dover was crowded, every steamer to Calais thronged with members of the aristocratic and leisured classes, who seemed to prefer Paris or even Nice out of season, to a city like London, where the police might act with such unexpected vigour … They had imagined that in 'the home of liberty' such practices passed unnoticed.[2]

Wilde had incensed his detractors during the libel trial by detaching art from morality and the writers of newspaper editorials were quick to make a connection between 'aesthetes' and sexual deviants; when the cross-examination moved to the dim-lit, perfumed rooms where the poet of the beautiful joined with valets and grooms in 'the bond of the silver cigarette case'.[3] Wilde was in the habit of bestowing such a gift on his lovers, its quality seemingly depending on the social status of the receiver. The *Westminster Gazette* attacked him for fastening art to 'the immoral, the morbid and the maniacal', branding him a hypocrite whose elevated boasting hid a degrading personal life.[4]

The two criminal trials (the first ended in an inconclusive verdict) proved to be pure gold for august and lurid publications alike. Sexual scandals in the eighties and early nineties involving establishment figures had fed the public's voyeuristic appetite. As the tale of Wilde's cuckoldry with working-class youths unfolded, something akin to rejoicing gripped the self-appointed guardians of public morality. The eventual guilty verdict, and the imposition of the maximum sentence of two years' imprisonment with hard labour, was widely applauded by the English press. *The Daily Telegraph* lauded the outcome as a stern rebuke to 'the artistic tendencies' of the time:

> We have had enough, and more than enough of Mr Oscar Wilde, who has been the means of inflicting upon public patience during the recent episode as much moral damage of the most offensive and repulsive kind as any single individual could well cause.[5]

And the *National Observer* trumpeted:

> There is not a man or woman in the English-speaking world possessed of the treasure of a wholesome mind who is not under a deep debt of gratitude to the Marquess of Queensberry for destroying the High Priest of the Decadents.[6]

Given the stigma attached to Wilde's behaviour, to defend him would have been social suicide. Even an attempt to save his reputation by distinguishing the man from the work would be equally fraught with the danger of guilt by association. Those who were brave enough to speak out confined themselves to questioning whether, after the widely publicised libel case and inconclusive first criminal trial, Wilde could ever have received a fair hearing; or in drawing attention to the disparity between Wilde's punishment and that meted out to men who corrupted girls. Ironically, one person who drew such a distinction was William Stead, the man largely responsible for precipitating the furore that had led to the 1885 Criminal Law Amendment Act. Stead attacked the double-standard that condemned Wilde but ignored the sexual exploitation of young girls and women by unscrupulous men:

> If Wilde, instead of indulging in dirty tricks of indecent familiarity with boys and men, had ruined the lives of half a dozen innocent simpletons of girls, or had broken up the home of his friend by corrupting his friend's wife, no one could have laid a finger upon him. The male is sacrosanct: the female is fair game. To have burdened society with a dozen bastards, to have destroyed a happy home by his lawless lust – of these things the criminal law takes no account. But let him act indecently to a young rascal who is very well able to take care of himself … then judges can hardly contain themselves from indignation when inflicting the maximum sentence the law allows … If all persons guilty of Oscar Wilde's offences were to be clapped into gaol, there would be a very surprising exodus from Eton and Harrow, Rugby and Winchester, to Pentonville and Holloway.[7]

Carpenter believed that Wilde was foolish to respond to Queensberry's goading, but when notices for his play *The Importance of Being Earnest* were removed from theatre billboards, in an anonymous letter to the *Star* he insisted that, when passing judgement on sexual behaviour, a clear distinction should be drawn between law and morality. He also penned a piece for the anarchist journal *Freedom*, criticising the 1885 Act for licencing blackmail, and defended the purity of homosexual relationships.[8] But not all in the socialist camp were as accommodating. The *Labour Leader*, mouthpiece of the Independent Labour Party, fastened this 'filthy abomination' to the idle rich.[9] *Justice*, the journal of the Social Democratic Federation took a more considered view, labelling it an acquired vice perpetrated in schools and the armed forces, which fuelled the demand for male prostitutes.[10]

In an act of defiance, Carpenter asked Stead if he would take the *Homogenic Love* pamphlet for the *Review of Reviews*, but Stead considered that its defence of male relationships was too overtly sexual. He made a further attempt to air the subject, telling Ellis: 'I have sent a paper entitled 'An Unknown People' to the *Humanitarian*, which I think they may insert',[11] but the editor declined to print it, although the journal later carried a review of the other pamphlets, the anonymous writer declaring: 'Believing as we do in the full and free discussion of questions which concern the moral, mental, physical and spiritual health of humanity, we are glad to extend a welcome to the efforts of this earnest and able seeker after truth'.[12]

Once imprisoned, Wilde sought a reduction of his sentence by cravenly describing his behaviour as a 'form of sexual madness', and pleaded to have himself put under medical care in order that 'the sexual insanity' from which he suffered might be cured. Other phrases that appeared in his petition were 'monstrous sexual perversion' and 'loathsome modes of erotomania'.[13] But once released, he fled to the continent and returned to his old mania of chasing after boys.

Wilde set indelibly in the public mind that homosexuality was male lust and nothing more. His appeal to the 'higher Philosophy' never reached beyond the courtroom in which the 'Professor of Aesthetics' enunciated it. From the golden youths of his own class, he descended to consort with unrefined, uneducated, 'renters'. His unbridled sexual satiation destroyed any claim he might have had to be the defender of homosexual love. It also reinforced the deep-seated prejudice that homosexual behaviour was a socially destructive vice. For many, seeking sexual pleasure with those of inferior social status was the greater offence; the mere association with such individuals being subversive of class hierarchy. The aristocratic Douglas's predatory lusting after working-class boys was even stronger than Wilde's. Carpenter was setting out to show the *normality* of the homosexual orientation, but at every turn Wilde and his cohorts kicked sand in his face. Together with his fellow 'aesthetes' and the Uranian poets (almost to an individual paederasts) he fixed in the public mind that homosexuality was about men corrupting boys and young men and nothing else. The insult 'oscarite' stuck.

Wilde's trial was the first of any prominent individual under the 1885 Act. It was a pointer to the establishment's nervousness that he was not prosecuted for sodomy, which carried a much harsher sentence. The renters who were to bring him down were unlikely to have agreed to testify had this been the charge, which would have inevitably left them facing the same fate. Charlie Parker, one of Wilde's sexual partners, in his deposition to Queensberry's solicitor, made no mention of sodomy, but under questioning during the criminal trial he freely admitted that Wilde had sodomised him. Arraigning Wilde with what was a *misdemeanou*r allowed his sexual partners to escape such a charge; in return for testifying for the prosecution. But, underlying this decision, must have been a fear that there might be a repeat of the Cleveland Street scandal that had ensnared individuals at the very pinnacle of the social pyramid. Then there was the decision not to prosecute Douglas. Letters in the National Archives indicate that this decision was made at the highest level. He was to be treated as a victim, corrupted by Wilde, against the clear evidence that he had willingly had sexual relations with several of the witnesses. Queensberry may have insisted that Douglas should not be prosecuted by threatening a bigger scandal involving senior members of the Liberal Government. Talk of a homosexual affair between his eldest son, Lord Drumlanrig, and Lord Roseberry, the Prime Minister, was widespread, leading Queensberry to conduct a scarcely concealed vendetta against him. Drumlanrig was killed in a shooting incident in October 1894, which looked suspiciously like suicide.[14]

As Carpenter described it, from the moment of Wilde's arrest, 'sheer panic prevailed over all questions of sex, and especially of course questions of the Intermediate Sex'.[15] Although he had not intended to include the *Homogenic Love* pamphlet in his book, copies had circulated quite widely and caused some fluttering and agitation in the dovecotes of Fleet Street. When the pamphlet came to the attention of Fisher Unwin, he got cold feet and wanted to back out of publishing the book:

> He wrote asking me for the HL pamphlet (which he had heard of) and when I saw him a day or two after, he wanted to wash his hands of me and all my works. Well he didn't say anything about TD [*Towards Democracy*] but about the others. I told him the others contained nothing about the HL subject, and that as for that subject, there was a panic about it in London just now, which would all pass away. However, he wouldn't listen and wanted me to cancel the agreement about the sex volume then and there. I refused to do that – but told him to reflect calmly on the whole matter and then write to me. He has not written yet, but of course it will be no good forcing him to publish if he does not want to. So you see the boycott has set in already. Isn't it a caution?[16]

In the end, Fisher Unwin cancelled the agreement. Even though a good part of the book had already been typeset, he was so anxious to be rid of it that he readily cut his losses, and went even further. Believing that it was dangerous to be the publisher of anything remotely sexual, in a final act of cleansing he turned out of his shop all remaining copies of *Towards Democracy* (which he had been selling for three years) and told him that he could not continue as his publisher. Carpenter told Ellis:

> I think there is no doubt that the H.L. pamphlet upset him. I guess he will try to get other publishers to boycott me! I have removed stock of T.D. to the Labour Press Manchester, and am going to work through them in future; meanwhile we are trying to get a London house to work with us. Have you any suggestions in this line? I want to get a London publisher or agent to work with the L.P. and then I would bring out T.D., the Sex-volume etc, through this channel. I hope you will get *your* arrangements fixed before long [a reference to *Sexual Inversion*]. How absurd it all is. It is very aggravating because it takes such a lot of time angling for these publishing fish and then playing them when hooked.[17]

He was determined to press on with the publication of the book, even though continuing with the project while Wilde languished in Reading Jail was obviously hazardous. Publishers were now fearful of a literary inquisition and to openly examine sex-relations clearly struck at the heart of many Victorians' sense of decency; while to put into print anything remotely concerned with homosexuality might be the death of a respectable publisher. In January 1896, Carpenter was commiserating with Ellis over his, so far, unsuccessful attempts to find a publisher for *Sexual Inversion*. 'What a panic there still is on the subject! Sometimes one feels depressed about it all. It seems as if one had just got the coffin-lid up a little way, and then down it comes again with a bang! But I believe in continuous and sustained forward pressure. We shall appear above ground some day'.[18]

He first offered the book to Swan Sonnenschein, which specialised in sociology and politics, but it was turned down, although the company took it six years later; by which time it was almost respectable. Five publishing houses declined to accept the book, with the then intended title *The Sexes in a Free Society*, before Bertram Dobell agreed to take the book, and to republish *Towards Democracy*. But in March, his plans were 'further decomposed' by the bursting of yet another publisher's bomb:

> Bertram Dobell, after settling everything with me about the publication of my two books, has now suddenly had a panic about my Homogenic pamphlet – of which he has heard, evidently an exaggerated account; and wants to throw it all up. What an arch fiend I must be! I have written to pacify him, but I almost fear in vain – in which case I shall have fresh arrangements to make and fresh delays.[19]

Dobell refused to listen to the voice of the charmer. The 'perfect panic' in London had finally reached all corners of the publishing world. There was no alternative but to shake the dust of London off his boots and fall back on the small Manchester Labour Press Society. Unwin's unsold copies of *Towards Democracy* were shipped there; a new title page was inserted and it was reissued. Shrewdly, he decided that the intended title for his new book should be changed to the less provocative, even charming, *Love's Coming of Age*, which was soon published by the Labour Press. At last, the first of his important sexual writings was out in book form, and even without a chapter on homosexuality, it was ground-breaking. Its subtitle was 'A Series of Papers on the Relations of the Sexes'.[20]

It was the first non-medical book published in England that explored the intricacies of gender, sexual, and marriage relationships. During his lifetime there would be twelve editions in England and seven in America, with French, German, Italian and Swedish translations. It established him as a significant popular writer on sexuality, but the book made its way into the world not through a host of welcoming reviews in established journals, but by word of mouth, largely within socialist and radical networks.

Despite the criticism of the book by modern-day feminists, it was given a particularly warm reception in radical women's circles. Apart from its elegant and witty dissection of bourgeois marriage codes, and its unqualified support for a new kind of womanhood, its frank exposition of sex as life-enhancing was a startlingly new outlook. Henry Salt, unwisely, claimed that Carpenter did not understand women, but reviewing the book for the *Labour Leader*, Lily Bell (Isobella Bream Pearce) praised him for having a deeper grasp than most men of the realities of women's lives, and for being one of the very few men who could 'write acceptably on matters of sex', especially in relation to women:

> Most men write with such an air of superiority, such an assumption of masculine authority and right to lay down the law as to what women may or may not do, what may or may not be her 'proper' sphere in life, that I usually take up their articles merely to lay them down again with a feeling of impatience and irritation ... I wish every man and woman in the country could give such books as this, a careful, thoughtful and earnest study.[21]

Olive Schreiner had earlier written from South Africa: 'The marriage pamphlet has come. I think it splendid'.[22] Ellis too, in his response to the pamphlet, recognised Carpenter's special talent for dealing with sexual topics in a non-medical way: 'I have read your Marriage paper with much satisfaction, and I like your argument, admiring the felicitous way in which you demolish the ordinary foolish quibbles, and also the calm and contemplative manner in which you view the whole proceedings'.[23] Now, he was equally impressed with the book: 'I have been looking at *Love's Coming of Age* – though not yet had time to read it properly

– I find it full of most beautiful things'.[24] Ellis was about to attend a medical conference in Russia and Carpenter asked him to take a copy with him as a gift for Tolstoy, who admired his writing on science. It travelled across European borders sown into the lining of Ellis's jacket, although circumstances intervened and it never reached Tolstoy.

Edith Ellis was overjoyed by the dropping of his 'sex bombs': 'It has come and I've read it and I'm real proud of you. It is a downright fine piece of work and worthy of you. It is most stimulating and clear and makes a body glad you're alive'.[25] Years later she wrote that few people realised at the time that it was a 'revolutionary' book. It held 'such unconventional suggestions for experiment in new sexual ethical living that one may almost classify it with Karl Marx's *Capital*, which held similar suggestions in the economical field'.[26] If her comparison with Marx was overdone, there had certainly never before been such a forthright condemnation of Victorian sexual codes, combined with a frank and open celebration of physical love.

He was especially pleased to receive Ellis's commendation: 'It is selling pretty well – though no doubt it would be better if we had a London publisher. To give you an idea – the *Literary World* refuses to insert an advertisement for it on the ground that the title looks rather suggestive!'[27] Meanwhile, he was looking forward to seeing the final proofs of *Sexual Inversion*.

Although the *Homogenic Love* pamphlet had not been included in *Love's Coming of Age*, Carpenter was determined to find an opening, at least for some of the material. When the furore over the Wilde trials had subsided, he resurrected his *An Unknown People* paper and asked Ellis if he could suggest who might take it: 'Any English magazine I suppose is hopeless; and in some ways I think I should prefer an American or International public'.[28] He was pleased, if surprised, when it was accepted by an English magazine, the *Reformer*, a leading liberal periodical. Its editorial stance was, that all opinions were to be 'freely admitted', as long as they were expressed 'reasonably and in proper language'. Carpenter was by now a consummate master of this art; well aware that he risked rejection if any provocative issues, such as the outright approval of same-sex physical intimacy, or a call for the reform of the 1885 Act, were discussed in the piece. The paper, which *was* published in two parts, was again ground-breaking; being the first defence of homosexuality to appear in England in a prominent journal with a national circulation. Later that year, the publisher issued it as a pamphlet.[29]

He had two audiences in mind. Firstly, he wanted to gain the sympathetic understanding of the intelligent layman; pointing out that individuals with a homosexual nature were not rare examples of a deviant sexuality but formed, if beneath the surface of society, a large group. A frank and open discussion of their situation should not be avoided. Society had a duty not only to understand them, 'but to help him to understand themselves'.[30]

> Anyone who realises what Love is, the dedication of the heart, so profound, so absorbing, so mysterious, so imperative, and always just in the noblest natures so strong, cannot fail to see how difficult, how tragic even, must often be the fate of those whose deepest feelings are destined from the earliest days to be a riddle and a stumbling-block, unexplained to themselves, passed over in silence by others.[31]

As this passage suggests, his second purpose was to give his own kind a feeling of self-worth and well-being. It was bad enough that they suffered inwardly because of their sexuality, without also suffering from the refusal of society to recognise their existence or to give them help. It was especially hard for the young; the veil of complete silence drawn over the subject led to painful misunderstandings and confusions of mind, with no recognition of 'the solitary and really serious inner struggles they may have to face'.[32]

Some key arguments from the *Homogenic Love* pamphlet are

repeated: the rejection of the morbidity thesis and support for the innateness of the homosexual orientation; the denial that such attachments are necessarily sexual, or connected with sexual acts. He knew that it was especially important to counteract the latter. To confuse homosexuals with libertines, 'having no law but curiosity in self-indulgence is to do them a great wrong'.[33]

PART THREE

15

A Scandalising Book

With London now galvanised by the Wilde trials, Carpenter saw danger ahead for Ellis's book. 'I'm afraid just now you will have difficulty in finding a publisher', he commiserated, but steeled Ellis against giving up the project: 'It is a difficult campaign, but by going on slowly twill all come right perhaps'. Some in Ellis's circle were advocating abandonment of the book but, in combative mood, Carpenter was 'glad to hear there is strong opposition to it in some quarters as that is always satisfactory'.[1]

In June, Ellis sent him the completed manuscript, which brought further encouragement: 'It is too silly about the publishers, but I think things will improve before long. I find all this stir has roused up the Urning community here & pulled it together a good deal'.[2] Ellis first offered the book to Williams and Norgate, a publishing house with a history of promoting scientific works, but it was rejected by its reader, who happened to be Ellis's friend, Dr Daniel Hack Tuke. Tuke advised the publisher that although the book was a specialist work aimed at the scientific community, given its subject matter it would be impossible to confine its circulation to such a readership, and there was a risk that it would come to the attention of the authorities. It was Tuke who made the memorable remark, 'There are always the compositors.[3] As a physician, Tuke shared the profession's distaste for the subject, and also, as a Quaker, did not favour the ventilation of sexual matters in public. He, 'could not possibly view sympathetically any detailed approach to the problems of sex.'[4] Moreover, his advice was likely to have been influenced by his close friendship with Symonds's father; inclining him to protect his memory. Later, as editor of the *Journal of Mental Science*, he published an anonymous critical review of the German edition, which may well have come from his own pen.

The atmosphere prevailing in the wake of the Wilde trials had probably extinguished any hope that a leading English publishing house would be prepared to risk prosecution by issuing a work that, *inter alia*, questioned the criminalisation of male homosexual relations conducted in private. After Williams and Norgate declined to take the book, Carpenter offered to get up a fund, if Ellis decided to publish the book at his own expense. Frustrated, although he wanted the book to appear initially in English, he did not take up Carpenter's offer. Instead, he asked his friend Dr Hans Kurella, a distinguished physician and anthropologist, if he would prepare a German translation. Given the greater acceptability there of publications on sexual subjects it made sense, and could pave the way for an English edition.

The Leipzig publisher, Wigand, issued it with the title, not altogether pleasing to Ellis, of *Das Konträre Geschlechtsgefül* (Contrary Sexual Feeling), with both Ellis's and Symonds's names on the title page. Carpenter was fulsome in his praise: 'Well done! … it will make a sensation when it comes out in England – there will be silence in heaven for half an hour'.[5]

Still looking for an English publisher, Ellis heard through a friend that a certain J. Astor Singer, 'a man of some wealth ... interested in scientific and philosophical subjects' was setting up a small publishing house, 'for the unostentatious issue of a few such works'. His agent in London was his brother-in-law, Dr Roland de Villiers, and an agreement to publish Ellis's book was 'speedily and easily arranged'.[6] But, unbeknown to Ellis, de Villiers was a swindler who had fled Germany, where he had been sentenced to twelve months' hard labour for forgery and other offences. As Ellis had wished, it was issued quietly under the fictitious trade name of 'Wilson and Macmillan'.[7] Its publication was only announced in prospectuses to doctors and lawyers and sent for review to a few medical and scientific journals.

Before the book could, in Carpenter's words, 'silence heaven', it was silenced from another quarter. From Venice, Horatio Brown had offered encouragement to Ellis, helped by providing case histories and read parts of the manuscript; which he admired for 'its calmness' and 'judicial unbiased tone', adding 'and if anything can persuade people to look the question in the face this should'.[8] He came back to London very soon after the book was out, to find that a number of Symonds's influential family friends were strongly advising suppression, on the ground that it would be injurious to his reputation and damage the family.

Brown was asked to halt distribution of the book, in order that Symonds's name could be removed from the title page and any material in the volume directly attributed to him taken out. A small number of copies had already been distributed but Brown bought up the remaining stock and had it destroyed. This first English edition was, therefore, never in general circulation. On learning of what had happened, Carpenter grumbled that there would be 'no trace of him left. Isn't it too silly – and a sheer betrayal of J.A.S'?[9] He wrote a letter of protest to Brown, who, in response, pleaded that he had been torn between loyalty to Symonds and respect for his family's wishes. The family's request had caused him 'great difficulty', and he resented the charge of acting unfairly to Symonds, pointing out that his place 'in the history of the controversy' was recorded in the German edition, 'which contains all he had to say, and more than Mr Ellis was prepared to publish in English'.[10]

> J.A.S. had all this matter by him for years, most of it, in print; the Problem in Greek Ethics was finished & published [this was done privately] more than ten years before his death and yet he never published it; never even put his name to the few copies he printed – this proves to me that he had at least grave doubts about publishing ... and I don't feel sure that he would have faced the inevitable anxiety and possible pain to his family.
>
> You probably do not know that the very last words he wrote, when he was past speech, and within a few hours of death, were a strong injunction to me to regard his family in all matters of publication. An appeal from one of his family; the strongly expressed opinion of his oldest and most intimate friends when I got to London, the best legal & medical opinion I could obtain, all combined to take the step I did: and though I may not have done quite what he would have liked (but did not do) I think I have done what he would have done in the circumstances.[11]

Symonds had certainly agonised over whether to publish any of his sexual writings; being bold in his determination to do so, and then drawing back when he thought about the likely consequences for his and his family's reputation. As he had known first-hand how Symonds had wavered, Brown's action was, on balance, justified. Carpenter, when he protested to Ellis, 'And what has he to do with the matter?', was unaware of how close Brown was to Symonds, who had taught him over twenty years earlier when he was a sixth-former at Clifton College.

The German edition had included a fair amount of Symonds's material that was not used in the English edition, being, in

Ellis's view, 'of minor importance'. The most substantial pieces attributed to him consisted of three appendices: the whole of his monograph *A Problem in Greek Ethics* (which they had agreed would merit a chapter); *Ulrichs'*, a chapter taken from the *Modern Problem*; *Notes on the Concubinus* – the practice of aristocratic young men permitted to consort sexually with slaves in ancient Rome. *There was also a letter from Professor X* (one sent to Symonds by James Mills Peirce, a Harvard professor of mathematics, arguing that homosexuality was normal and not immoral). In the main text, there were four brief references to Symonds, together with ten footnotes. Without a meticulous comparative analysis, it is not possible to identify what Ellis, if at all, took from the *Modern Problem* and wove seamlessly into the text.

He acknowledged that the finished result was not what his collaborator had wished for. It was 'somewhat more shapeless than it was planned to be, and Mr Symonds's part in it, which would otherwise have been fitted into the body of the book, mostly appears as fragmentary appendices'.[12] He added that he did not think the essay on Greek homosexuality threw 'any great light on sexual inversion as a congenital psychic abnormality'.[13] Strictly speaking this was true, but it should be stressed that Symonds would never have agreed that ethnography had nothing to contribute to the understanding of homosexuality. It was not sufficient to show that congenital homosexuality was not a perversion. He had wanted, as Ellis clearly understood, a unified work which synthesised scientific, ethnographic and historical material. He saw this as a critical part of the case for legal reform, deeper than Ellis's purely utilitarian arguments. Without the contribution that he had anticipated making, it was not a comprehensive account of homosexuality. Such a treatment would have been innovative, and distinguished it from the work of continental writers. It could have educated the general public and better challenged the existing law governing male-on-male sexual relations.

With minimal editing, and no significant rewriting, Ellis was easily able to remove all traces of Symonds and produce a new English edition. Having recast the work, he told Carpenter: 'In some ways the change will be an improvement, and it certainly renders it safe from attacks of all kind',[14] an assumption that would soon be shattered. As no other leading London publisher could be found to take the book, Ellis, seemingly still unaware of de Villiers's background, again turned to him. An expensive linotype printing plant had been built at Watford and it was published there, using a second fictitious trade name.[15] When the new edition appeared, Carpenter was full of praise:

> I think it so fine – one of the best things that you have done – clear and balanced – yet leading to definite conclusions ... It is (I think) the best scientific treatment of the subject wh [*sic*] I have seen. And the character of your cases (their healthiness &c.) gives a special value to the book. I now feel that the subject has got a hearing and expression in England.[16]

The book had again been issued quietly, with notices posted to suitable recipients, mainly doctors and lawyers, and review copies sent to the medical and scientific journals. But one organisation that acquired copies was the Legitimation League, a radical society for the promotion of sexual reforms, including the legalising of illegitimate children. Promoting free love, it was also sympathetic to same-sex relationships, recognising 'the absolute freedom of two individuals of full age, to enter into and conclude at will, any mutual relationships whatever, where no third person's interests are concerned'.[17] The League had, for some time, been of interest to the police as an organisation with aims that were seen to threaten public morals, and as a haunt of subversives. John Sweeney, an under-cover police officer posing as an anarchist, began attending meetings of the League and won the confidence of its secretary, George Bedborough, who was selling copies of the League's publications and various books, including *Sexual Inversion*. Sweeney purchased a copy, before revealing his true identity. Bedborough was then charged with selling an obscene book.

A shocked Ellis was advised to obtain legal advice but was not arrested, as the real objective of the police operation was not the prosecution of his book but the destruction of the Legitimation League. News of the impending prosecution quickly led to the setting up of a Free Press Defence Committee, to which several leading figures of the day lent their names. George Bernard Shaw penned an indignant letter of support, complaining that the attempt to place an authoritative scientific book beyond the reach of those who could not read German was 'a masterpiece of police stupidity and magisterial ignorance'.[18] Letters of support came from distinguished American and European psychologists and physicians. The translator of the German edition, Hans Kurella, wrote: '[T]he whole of scientific psychology and medicine on the Continent is on your side'.[19] But in England, not a single doctor of prominence supported it, and the *Lancet*, the leading medical journal, declined to review it. Ellis's mistake, it pontificated, was to allow a book containing such material to enter the everyday world, instead of going to a publishing house 'able to take proper measures for introducing it as a scientific book to a scientific audience'.[20] The general public had to remain ignorant of homosexuality and any advance towards a wider understanding of it quickly extinguished. For the clergy, it was anathema. William Inge, the then Dean of St Paul's, allegedly threw his copy on the fire. More surprising, was the reaction of women who were to be at the forefront of the fight to have control over their bodies. Marie Stopes likened reading it to 'breathing a bag of soot', and Margaret Sanger, whose book on birth control was prosecuted in America, recoiled from the long accounts of what was regarded as homosexual indulgence found in the histories.[21]

The case was set down to be heard at the Central Criminal Court. The following extracts from the indictment vividly illustrate the horror of homosexuality that informed the extraordinary drafting:

> George Bedborough being a person of wickedly depraved mind and disposition, and unlawfully and wickedly devising, contriving and intending to vitiate and corrupt the morals of the liege subjects of our said Lady the Queen, to debauch and poison the minds of divers of the liege subjects of our said Lady the Queen, and to raise and create in them lustful desires, and to bring the said liege subjects into a state of wickedness, lewdness and debauchery ... unlawfully, wickedly, maliciously, scandalously, and wilfully, did publish, sell and utter, and cause and procure to be published, sold and uttered a certain lewd, wicked, bawdy, scandalous and obscene libel, in the form of a book entitled Studies in the Psychology of Sex: Vol.1. Sexual Inversion by Havelock Ellis, in which said book are contained among other things, divers wicked, lewd, impure, scandalous and obscene libels, and matters, which said book is, pursuant to the provisions in that behalf, of the Law of Libel Amendment Act, 1888.

The Defence Committee briefed Horace Avory, a brilliant young barrister, to defend Bedborough on a plea of not guilty. He, unsuccessfully, sought to have the case heard in the High Court, on the ground that it was a scientific book that should be considered by a superior judge and jury. He was unaware that the authorities were already working behind the scenes to ensure that the book would never be ventilated in public.

In preparing a defence of the book, Ellis swore the following affidavit:

> The said book was written by me as the result of many years' scientific study, investigation and observation and was written

purely in the interests of science and scientific investigation and to the best of my ability in a scientific spirit. The said work is the first volume of a series of works which I am engaged in writing being studies in the psychology of sex. It deals with the subject of sexual abnormalities and in order to properly treat of these matters from a scientific point of view and to arrive at a conclusion with regard to the remedies for the practises dealt with (which frequently lead to crime, disease and insanity) it has been necessary to instance cases which have actually occurred. The matter has been treated to the best of my ability in the least possible objectionable manner and with the sole object of elucidating the truth and arriving at a satisfactory conclusion as to remedial treatment. The general scope and objects of the book appears from the prefaces and also from the concluding chapter and I crave to refer to those portions of the book on those points.

He must have been advised by his counsel that he should stress strongly the medical importance of the book, because he palpably contradicted two of its conclusions: that homosexuality was not a morbid condition and that, in such cases, no 'remedial treatment' would be effective.

But a defence of the book would not be required, as before the case went to court the police had put pressure on Bedborough. Unless he agreed to plead guilty, they would reveal embarrassing details about his unorthodox family life, but if he co-operated, he would escape a prison sentence. This would be a satisfactory outcome for both sides, with no scandalising trial. It was sufficient that the book should be banned and the Legitimation League destroyed. Bedborough, who was also indicted on ten other counts connected with articles published in *The Adult*, duly pleaded guilty before the Recorder of London, Sir Charles Hall, who warned him:

So long as you do not touch this filthy work again with your hands and so long as you lead a respectable life, you will hear no more of this. But if you choose to go back to your evil ways, you will be brought up before me, and it will be my duty to send you to prison for a very long time.[22]

Bedborough was bound over and fined £100. Except for the appearance of his name in the indictment, no mention was made of Ellis during the short hearing. As no charge of publishing an obscene libel had been brought against him personally, and because of Bedborough's guilty plea, the book was never defended in open court. It may well be that, for Ellis, this was the best outcome. It is difficult to see how his counsel could have defended the book without calling him as the principal witness, which might well have destroyed him, given his extreme nervousness when having to speak in public. Under cross-examination, the veracity of his case histories, on which the whole book was constructed, and where its 'obscenity' really lay, would have been pivotal. But, except for the cases of Carpenter, Symonds and Edith Ellis, he knew none of his respondents personally, and for their authenticity had to rely entirely on those who had provided them. How could he have spoken with authority?

Given the entrenched attitudes towards homosexuality, and hostility from the medical profession, it is doubtful whether *Sexual Inversion* could ever have been successfully defended as an important scientific book worthy of public dissemination. Until 1935 in England, only medical practitioners could legally possess it. But once it was labelled scandalous and obscene, a clandestine demand for the work was immediately created.

If relieved of the ordeal of appearing in the witness box, Ellis was severely shaken by the verdict. This totally unexpected setback to his progress had revealed a certain naivety on his part, as he recognised years later. Lacking Carpenter's cunning, he had supposed that a secluded student approaching his subject with precaution; making no direct appeal to the general public but only to the public's teachers; who wrapped up the results of his inquiries in a technically written volume open to few, would be secure from attack. He was only forty years old at the time, but the event was a turning point in his life, 'even the chief-turning point'; the end of the upward climb and the beginning of what he felt to be a descent. 'Until then, although I always looked older than my age, I had retained an instinctive feeling of youthfulness ... But now, somehow, this instinctive feeling was suddenly and forever killed. I realised that I was no longer young'.[23]

He wrote a small pamphlet about the book's prosecution, which was printed in America. It was an uncompromising statement of his steely determination not to be diverted from his course. He was an impartial student whose path in life he had long marked out. He would leave to others the task of wrestling in the public arena for the freedom to publish work concerned with sexual life. It was not a task that he had ever contemplated for himself, and he did not intend to injure his work, or distort his vision of life, by entering upon such a struggle:

> The pursuit of the martyr's crown is not favourable to the critical and dispassionate investigation of complicated problems. A student of nature, of men, of books may dispense with wealth or position: he cannot dispense with quietness and serenity. I insist on doing my own work in my own way, and cannot accept conditions which make this work virtually impossible.[24]

It had been a crushing blow to discover that his own country refused him the basic conditions of intellectual freedom. His book dealt with the facts of English life, and he wished to address English people. This opportunity having been denied him, in 1901 he transferred the publication of future books to America. He never forgot, or forgave, this attack on freedom of expression and the suppression of scientific knowledge. As he put it, 'the mighty engines of Social Order and Respectability' were set in motion to crush its publication.[25]

Given the historical importance of the book, how is Ellis's support, or otherwise, for the homosexual to be judged? In the division of labour for the intended joint-publication Symonds had been given the task of writing the conclusion. The form that this should take; whether it was to be a summary of the book's principal conclusions or something else, was never discussed. In the event, much of what Ellis wrote under the heading 'Conclusions' would have been rejected by Symonds. It was not a summing up of the book's main findings but a chapter that opened with the topic 'The Prevention of Homosexuality'.

Ellis's often-stated objective was to examine human sexuality in the round; dispassionately, without stigmatising any particular form of its expression. His sympathy for the homosexual, expressed in letters to Symonds and Carpenter, and no doubt influenced by his wife's lesbianism, seemed genuine enough. However, he urged the male homosexual to come to terms with his abnormal sexual attraction and to refrain from physical intercourse: '[S]elf-restraint and self-culture, without self-repression, seems to be the most rational method of dealing with sexual inversion when that condition is really organic and deep-rooted'.[26] This assertion exposed Ellis's lack of contact with homosexual men, or any real understanding of their psychological and physical needs. It also set aside the statements of many of the individuals who made up his cases. Given the rigid taboo against homosexuality, *self-repression* was almost inevitable.

Ellis wrote that Symonds 'is quite certain that he suffers or benefits in health of mind and body according as he abstains from or indulges in moderate homosexual pleasure'.[27] When he began to express his inborn homosexual instincts he rapidly recovered his health. His neurotic disturbances subsided and his chronic lung disease was, at least, alleviated. Ellis observed: 'Coitus with males ... always seems to him healthy and natural; it leaves a deep sense of well-being, and has cemented durable friendships'.[28] And in a number of other cases where individuals had come to accept their condition without moral misgivings, sexual relations were said to improve mental and physical health.

Such statements must have made it very clear to Ellis that the repression of all sexual desire was harmful, yet there was to be no outlet for the release of the homosexual's sexual energy except for nocturnal dreams and solitary masturbation. Instead, it was 'the ideal of chastity, rather than of abnormal sexuality which the congenital invert should hold before his eyes'. It was necessary to 'refine and spiritualise' the sexual impulse in order that 'the invert's natural perversion may not become a cause of acquired perversity in others'.[29]

He concluded his account of homosexuality by asking his reader what the 'reasonable attitude' of society should be towards the congenital sexual invert. His own view was that his behaviour had to be subject to some form of social control: 'We are bound to protect the helpless members of society against the invert.' But 'we should not seek to destroy him before he has sinned against society'. This would be 'to exceed the warrant of reason'. After all, he was not an entirely worthless individual and, in trying to eliminate him, 'we may, perhaps, destroy also those children of the spirit who possess sometimes a greater worth than the children of the flesh'.[30] It says a great deal about his lack of understanding of the impact of being homosexual, and his reluctance to discuss it, that when individuals who had managed to acquire a copy of *Sexual Inversion* wrote to him, he invariably suggested that they should consult Carpenter. He noted that the chief effect of attempts to suppress homosexuality had been to arouse 'the finer minds among sexual inverts to undertake the enthusiastic defence of homosexuality'.[31]

A further blow was dealt when Ellis turned to the issue of marriage and the fathering of children. He was well aware that many men with a homosexual drive, like Symonds, had married and fathered healthy children. However, if there was no 'cure' for sexual inversion, it was undesirable that the invert should possess the power of reproduction:

> Often, no doubt, the children [of inverts] turn out very well, but for the most part they bear witness that they belong to a neurotic and failing stock. Sometimes, indeed, the tendency to sexual inversion in eccentric and neurotic families seems merely to be Nature's merciful method of winding up a concern which, from her point of view, has ceased to be profitable.[32]

He had promised that he would make his cases the kernel of his book, but in reaching a judgement on the role of heredity, as with the issue of physical love-making, he ignored what they revealed. Of the twenty-seven males, only one, a physician, believed that his homosexuality was hereditary. Fourteen reported that their parents or ancestors were healthy, whilst five made no mention of parentage or ancestry. A final group was made up of seven individuals who believed that a relative was, or may have been, homosexual, but parents or ancestors were either recorded as healthy or not mentioned.

He, chose not to repudiate the still entrenched view that homosexuality was linked to heredity; together with a number of mental and physical disorders that could be traced in family histories. His stance would have pained Symonds, the father of four highly intelligent and perfectly normal girls. Several of the individuals who had provided Symonds with their histories were men of high intellectual and cultural achievement who had married and fathered healthy children. As homosexuality was congenital, Symonds observed, '[e]very family runs the risk of producing a boy or girl whose life will be embittered by inverted sexuality, but who in all other respects will be no worse or better than the normal members of the home'.[33]

Since the publication of Francis Galton's influential *Hereditary Genius*,[34] the study of the factors amenable to social control which could influence the physical and mental qualities of future generations had gained force. Ellis accepted many of Galton's ideas and would become a vice-president of the Eugenics Education Society. In his book *The Task of Social Hygiene*, he wrote:

> Eventually, it seems evident, a general system, whether private
> or public, whereby all personal facts, biological and mental,
> normal and morbid, are duly and systematically registered,
> must become inevitable if we are to have a real guide as to those
> persons who are most fit, or most unfit, to carry on the race.[35]

And in a 1922 collection of essays, he wrote: 'We can seldom be absolutely sure what stocks should not propagate ... but we can attain reasonable probability, and it is on such probabilities in every department of life that we are always called upon to act'.[36] He concluded:

> But it is not only our right, it is our duty, or rather, one may
> say, the natural impulse of every rational and humane person,
> to seek that only such children may be born as will be able to
> go through life with a reasonable prospect that they will not
> be heavily handicapped by inborn defect or special liability to
> some incapacitating disease.[37]

Ellis's position fits with this last assertion, confirming that he never entirely detached himself from a hereditarian position on homosexuality.

Finally, when he turned to the clause in the 1885 Criminal Law Amendment Act that, with the exception of buggery, had made any sexual act between males a *misdemeanour*, it was not to give support to the sexual liberation of the homosexual. Like many who did not approve of homosexuality, Ellis believed that the clause would have been in harmony with the most enlightened

European legislation had the law not made homosexual acts that took place in private an offence. He repeated the view of those seeking reform, that the law should be confined to the protection of minors and the preservation of public order. As he regarded the practice of homosexuality to be socially undesirable, which was the overwhelming view of the Victorians, it is only in the legal sphere, and on utilitarian not moral grounds, that he could be said to have challenged it. As he asserted, he was confident that in England, 'social opinion, law or no law, will speak with no uncertain voice' on the acceptability of homosexuality.[38]

Several editions of *Sexual Inversion* were published, in which substantial new material was introduced; much to take account of Magnus Hirschfeld's findings[39] and Iwan Bloch's encyclopaedic studies of sexuality.[40] And in the new era initiated by Freud, he had to reconcile his work with claims that homosexuality, rather than being a congenital abnormality was an acquired behaviour. Being an empiricist to his core, he doubted whether the psychological mechanism posited by Freud could ever be demonstrated

He introduced new material examining so-called treatments by hypnotism, associational therapy and psychoanalysis, concluding that none offered a 'cure'. The 'ideal of chastity' remained his recommendation for the homosexual intent on happiness. This was the path through which, he claimed, most of the more highly intelligent men and women whose histories he had recorded had 'reached a condition of relative health and peace, both physical and moral'.[41] He ignored the fact that in most of his histories the very opposite was claimed. He was content to repeat his statement from the first English edition: 'I am inclined to say that if we can enable an invert to be healthy, self-restrained, and self-respecting, we have often done better than to convert him into the mere feeble simulacrum of a normal man'.[42]

The expression of such opinions makes it difficult to support the view that he was the first investigator 'to grant them [homosexuals] dignity as complete human beings',[43] or that he had set out to present a case for homosexuality by broadening the spectrum of acceptable sexual behaviour, presenting it as an innocuous departure from the sexual norm.[44] It has also been claimed that Ellis anticipated 'a sexual Elysium, where all types of sexual impulse could be expressed – including homosexuality',[45] a view inconsistent with what he wrote. Indeed, as shown, he went beyond disapproving of homosexual practices to actively discouraging them. Although not opposed to the repeal of legislation that penalised homosexual behaviour in private, at the same time he denied the male homosexual the consummation of his love.

Having completed his examination of homosexuality, with an evident weariness and a veiled self-judgement on the wisdom of having undertaken such a study, he was keen to move on: 'We have not wasted our time in this toilsome excursion. With the knowledge here gained we are the better equipped to enter upon the study of the wider questions of sex'.[46]

Although he abandoned scientific objectivity when he made moral judgements about the homosexual and the practice of homosexuality, his place as a sexual modernist is beyond dispute. His aim was to free the study of human sexuality from the Victorian straight-jacket in which it had been confined. His studies helped to establish some of the basic descriptive categories of sexual phenomena that would inform subsequent research. Above all, he reinforced the scientific underpinning that the study of sexuality required. The empirical foundations that he helped to lay have never been significantly dislodged.

16

A Journey to the East

In February 1890, Carpenter spent a few days in Cambridge, lodging at King's and hardly venturing into Trinity Hall, except to dine with Andrew Beck and play games with his five children. Beck had certainly risen, for he was now the Master of the college.

In a revealing unpublished note, probably written soon after his return home, he vividly relived the turmoil of his life there:

> Five and twenty years ago an undergraduate, a mere freshman I wandered thro [*sic*] these gardens – the thrushes calling as now, the smell of the dead leaves still lingering under the great Trinity Hall chestnuts ... full of vague longings, aspiration, emotion; or came down and stood at night upon the terrace over the river, in the profound hush and silence ... stood long & long, all strange and wonderful to me – sexual & religious thoughts and desires inextricably mingled in my mind. Vague, with vast possibilities, tensions, wonderment.

What agitations, what inner turmoil beneath outer calm, what longings occupying the whole background of life! The figures and faces of friends poignant with what attractions, filling one with passions one dared not speak, faintly reciprocated pursing night and day; the rest and refuge from them in hard boating and reading, the lovely confidences & tendernesses, the long walks thro [*sic*] unfrequented fields, the breakfast and wine parties with immense disputations & arguments (always rather wearisome to me) – all this framed in the beautiful setting of the place itself.

He sensed that some of the 'restraints' that had driven him from the place had vanished. There was something 'richer, more friendly, affectionate, far-reaching' in the characters of the young fellows, much less of the intellectual sharpness and epigrammatic display in conversation which had invariably passed for personal distinction in his own time there. 'I felt nearer to them than I used to feel even to those of my own day'.[1]

He confided to Oates: 'I have been wonderfully happy and contented lately – too much so almost, for I am afraid it forebodes storms! – sailing along enjoying just what fare Destiny has served up'.[2] He was on the crest of a wave. His new book, *Civilisation*, had recently been published, and like much of his work it was an exhalation, an expurgation. After almost every book that followed the first part of *Towards Democracy*, he found himself feeling inwardly stronger, whilst somewhat indifferent to its reception. He always wrote more for himself than for public acclamation, 'for my own satisfaction as much as for the sake of others'.[3] If inwardly happier, he was restless. He grumbled about the long gloomy English winter and yearned for a place where there was an abundance of sunshine: 'I sometimes think I shall go off to India or some distant region before long – not for good! – but to renovate my faith, and unfold the frozen buds which civilisation and fog have nipped'.[4]

159

Little over a year earlier, Ponnambalam Arunachalam, his friend from his Cambridge days, had written from Ceylon (now Sri Lanka): 'Oh that you were here to commune with the only man I have known who is a seer and not one blindly groping in the dark'. He was speaking of his newly found Gnāni or wise man. He had a simple message for Carpenter: 'Come to the East and seek the truth'.[5] The following year he returned to the subject, chiding him for delaying. He had now read *Civilisation*: 'You are steadily working your way to Saiva (the essence of the ancient religions of India) in comparison with which other religions are mere child's play and trifling ... it alone will harmonise your now conflicting theories and your ideals with your practice'.[6] In the face of such insistence, he surrendered to Ponnambalam's entreaties: 'I had, indeed dreamed of such a recontre and had felt a persuasion that the dream was destined to be fulfilled'. It would be an opportunity to study this ancient cult of divine knowledge, which he felt to be 'something wonderful, a centuries-long tradition of facts about birth and death, and the soul's union with God'.[7]

He left for Colombo in the middle of October 1890, and planned not to return until the following March, happily abolishing the English winter altogether. He was hastened on his way by an ever-affectionate George Hukin, who was now acting as a self-appointed amanuensis during Carpenter's frequent absences from Millthorpe. George urged him to write before he arrived in Colombo. 'You'll have plenty of time on the ship, and I shall really long to hear from you'.[8] The bond between them always seemed to strengthen when he was away.

In taking up Ponnambalam's entreaty to act as a mediator between East and West, he was determined to return with more than impressions that would live on only in his own memory. He would make fulsome notes, recording scenes of nature and of ordinary human life among all classes of native society. It was in the lives of the mass people of this vast continent that he hoped to find a greater assurance of his belief in the essential oneness of humanity. [9]

On board the *Kaiser Wilhelm* he befriended a Singhalese crew-member, Kuala, a former dancer, handsome and 'remarkably well-made and powerful'.[10] Carpenter would be welcomed into Kuala's family and he would act as guide and chaperone during his stay in Ceylon. Disembarking in Colombo, he was immediately drawn to the idyllic scenery; the little thatched cottages plastered with mud, and the Singhalese and Tamil men in their brightly coloured clothes. He found their physicality entrancing, with some 'very nice-looking men' among them, with next to no garments on, thronging the roads with their bullock carts and working in the fields. All that he surveyed affirmed that there were 'beautiful things in the world and hope yet'.[11] He felt an immediate affinity with the land and its people and was soon telling the Salts: 'I am quietly taking root here and soaking down into it all ... As to the heat it is just nice – one wears cotton things merely for decency's sake as they say – nothing is really required'.[12] He readily took to the diet of plentiful rice and curry, bananas and pineapples.

For several weeks, with Arunachalam acting as interpreter, he saw the Gnāni nearly every day – he generally sitting on his couch dressed only in a white muslin wrap wound loosely round his form, with bare arms and feet. Only a question was required for him to launch into a long discourse, interspersed with vivid illustrations and digressions, but always returning to the point. The Gnāni might maintain his discourse for hours with unflagging concentration, after which he would 'return to that state of interior meditation and absorption in the contemplation of the world disclosed to the inner sense, which had apparently become his normal condition'.[13]

In the Gnāni, 'in some respects a high type of pre-civilization man', he felt that he had come into contact with 'the root thought of all existence – the intense *consciousness* (not conviction merely) of the oneness of all life – the germinal idea which in one form or another … [had] become the soul and impulse of religion after religion'.[14] He had found 'the amazing representative of the same spirit in all its voluminous modern unfoldment' in Whitman. The visit to the Eastern sage, was like 'going back to the pure lucid intensely transparent source of some mighty and turbulent stream'.[15]

Reluctantly bidding farewell to the Arunachalams, he took the boat to the Indian mainland and over several weeks, Madras, Calcutta, Delhi and Bombay were visited. In each there was a wealth of things to be recorded and remembered: sights, scenes, and the hubbub of the teeming crowds. His ascent of the mountain Adam's Peak in Ceylon, to view a shrine near the peak, claimed both by Hindus and Buddhists, was later matched towards the end of his stay in India by a visit to the Island of Elephanta to view its famous caves and Hindu shrines. They symbolised the beginning and the end of what had been a kind of pilgrimage.

On a beautiful day in early March, he stood at the rail of the *Siam*, as it slipped its moorings and steamed out into Bombay harbour. He savoured a final sight of the variegated shore, the small picturesque passing islands and the numerous colourful small craft that danced across the ship's bows. He did not wish to remind himself that Millthorpians were likely to be shivering under a leaden March sky and driving north-east winds. He went down to his berth to rest and when he went back on deck the ship was far out of sight of land. At night he stood for long periods at the ship's rail, the warm wind upon his face and its scented aroma in his nostrils. Looking up, he thought of his days teaching astronomy, vainly trying to catch a glimpse of the heavens on a smoke-wreathed moor. In the crystal-clear canopy, could be seen Canopus and the Southern Cross and Milky Way, forming a great radiance in the south. Far ahead to the west Orion lay on his side, and Sirius and the ruddy Aldebaran setting were clearly visible. As he stood in the pitch darkness, there was nothing between him and this immense world; nothing to even show that the ship was moving, except the rush of water as it ploughed forward. The whole of his journey, he later reflected, had been like this, 'so smooth, so unruffled, as if one had not really been moving'; as if he had not left home at all and it had been only 'a fair panorama that had been gliding past one all these months'.[16] When he reached London, he was half glad to be back. He had missed his friends a great deal, while England was certainly one of the most beautiful countries in the world, if only there was a little more sun.

Some years later, he acknowledged the significance of this journey for his future life:

> The visit to the East in some sense completed the circle of my experiences. It took two or three years for its results to soak and settle into my mind; but by that time I felt that my general attitude towards the world was not likely to change much, and that it only remained to secure and define what I had got hold of and to get it decently built out if possible into actual life and utterance'.[17]

It was not long after his return that his extensive notes were given book form as From *Adam's Peak to Elephanta*. It *was* a very unconventional 'travel guide'; remarkably discerning in what it brought vividly to life. It was held together by an impressive erudition and infused by his abiding political and social ideals. A large part was devoted to a critical, and witty, parody of the British in India; behaving as if the natives did not exist.

The book would later provoke another feminist's attempt to undermine Carpenter, by claiming that the book was imbued with homoerotic desire; that his enthusiasm for the East was entrenched in the nineteenth-century convention of homosexual Orientalism.[18] The *Bhagavad Gita*, which consecrates the love of the warrior Arjuna for the youthful demi-god Krishna, is amenable to homoerotic interpretation, and Carpenter recognised that 'the worship of sex is found to lie at the root of the present Hinduism, as it does at the root of nearly all the primitive religions of the world'.[19] However, there is little doubt, after his protracted correspondence with Arunachalam, that the motivating force for his visit was spiritual. It was oriental religion, not sex, that drew him to the East.

Bakshi wrote that Carpenter was guilty of 'sexual colonialism' in his treatment of Ceylon and India, and that there was a 'powerful personal erotic subtext' in the book.[20] But there is little in the book that links him to a tradition of nineteenth-century English homosexual literature, in which the Orient is represented as a region free of the constraints of Western sexual taboos. Carpenter's physical descriptions of boys and men do not amount to a homoerotic fixation. Their semi-nakedness, dictated by their status as peasants and the climate, would naturally mean that they were not inhibited about their bodies, in contrast to the over-dressed Europeans. Carpenter took his well-known views on the healthiness of nudity with him, and he nowhere portrays oriental males as 'free of emotional constraints … and potentially available for sexual liaisons'. [21] Moreover, there is nothing in the work that supports her claim that he endeavoured to formulate an Oriental ideal of male beauty, equivalent to one found in classical art and literature. There are passages, here and there, which anticipate his, soon to be declared, views on sexual liberation, but it is the life of the people, in all its rich variety, and his critical assessment of the British Raj, which are at the centre of the work, not a preoccupation with oriental sexuality.

17

A Lasting Love

Shortly after his return from India, he was on a train when a group of young men got into his carriage. One of them, twenty-four-year-old George Merrill, good-looking with a slender, supple figure, immediately caught his eye. They exchanged a few polite words and a look of recognition passed between them; a lingering of the eyes that steals beyond a glance and which among lovers of their own sex carries a peculiar intimacy and unspoken understanding.[1]

When he left the train, he joined up with a group of fellow travellers walking home. Casually glancing back, he saw that George had left his friends and was following at a distance. He felt a thrill of anticipation: 'His appealing look even at that distance reached me'.[2] After a little manoeuvring he managed to drop behind his party and George caught up with him. He immediately blurted out that he had noticed him several times in Sheffield and had harboured a burning desire to know him. Boldly, he implored him to stop and let the others go on. A flustered Carpenter resisted George's entreaties, but before they

165

parted he had secured his name and his address in Sheffield. So began a relationship which became almost immediately close and intimate, and which would span thirty-seven years.

This fortuitous meeting was between a lovesick man entering middle-age, excited and flattered by the attention of an attractive, sexually provocative individual twenty-three years his junior. He could not have met an individual whose whole nature and personality was so different from his own. This contrast would be a large part of George's appeal; apart from his brimming sexuality, he was utterly untouched by 'the prevailing conventions and proprieties of the upper world'.[3]

At first glance, George was not the sought-after lover. Quite the opposite. His 'ideal of love', Carpenter had revealed to Havelock Ellis, was 'a powerful, strongly built man, of my own age or rather younger – preferably of the working class'.[4] In *Towards Democracy*, this ideal appears in the form of 'the thick-thighed hot course-fleshed young bricklayer with the strap round his waist'; the 'good-natured fair-haired Titan at work in the fields', and the engine stoker, 'lusty with well-knit loins'. He had found such an embodiment in the person of George Hukin. But in Merrill he found 'the spontaneity, closeness to the earth and devotion that, while struggling against his bourgeois upbringing, he had always craved'.[5] He was to get affection in abundance from a young man by temperament loving and passionate, who could satisfy his 'imperious need for mutual nearness or contact, as to sleep naked with a naked friend'.[6]

George was exclusively homosexual and attracted to 'strong and mature men'. A skilful seducer, he moved confidently within the homosexual underworld, uninhibited and incautious, as his boldness in 'picking up' Carpenter showed. His good looks, affectionate disposition and powerful sex-drive brought him frequent success. He was the 'shameless lusty unpresentable pal' celebrated in *Towards Democracy*, inhabiting the 'unrespectable' world beyond the middle-class pale.

George was 'intensely feminine in character'. As a child he clung to his mother, helping her to sow quilts, knit stockings and make skirts for dolls.[7] Carpenter had told Ellis: 'Anything *effeminate* in a man ... repels me decisively'.[8] But *femininity* was altogether different because it crossed gender. As he would write: 'the inner psychical affections and affinities shade off and graduate, in a vast number of instances, most subtly from male to female'.[9] Others did not make such a fine distinction between effeminacy and femininity. Magnus Hirschfeld, who had met George at Millthorpe, claimed that he was privately referred to as 'Gorgette'.[10]

The large age-gap between them would make the relationship more akin to that of father and son, which was clearly expressed in the small number of letters that passed between them. The salutations, 'My Dear Faithful Dad' and 'My Dearest Dad' are used frequently by George, and Carpenter would tell Charles Oates: 'I feel a great tenderness towards him, as to a son'.[11]

He expressed his paternal feelings towards him in one of the most simple and beautiful of his poems, *Hafiz to the Cupbearer*. It includes the lines:

Dear Son, that out of the crowded footways of Shiraz,
With hesitant step emerging,
Camest and laid thy life down at my feet ...
I take thy gift, so gracious and sparkling-clear,
Thy naive offering, as of a simple Nature-child ...
Come, son (since thou hast said it), out of all Shiraz
Hazif salutes the comrade. Let us go
A spell of life along the road together.[12]

George was one of nine children raised in poverty in the Sheffield slums, 'a child of the gutter'. He went out to work at the age of thirteen and had a series of jobs: giving out towels in a bathhouse, fetching and carrying for moulders and casters, and driving a horse and cart for a file-grinder. When he was seventeen, he became a barman and waiter in a pub, replacing his earlier ill-paid monotonous toil with a life peppered by drunken customers and smutty jokes. Moving on, he became an assistant to an itinerant encyclopaedia salesman and spent three months in Scarborough, where he had a number of sexual liaisons. There was an elderly aristocratic gentleman who wanted to take him away as his kept-boy, and a handsome younger man with Mediterranean looks, who Merrill dubbed his 'Italian count'.

Later, working in York, he had a short 'affair' that revealed how such encounters easily crossed the class divide, uniting in sexual desire the high and the low. One day he found himself at the railway station when the Prince of Wales arrived with an entourage, to take a train to nearby Tranby Croft. Merrill's account is so illuminating of such encounters that it is worth relating in full:

Of course, they were all very smart with frock coats and tall hats and flowers in their buttonholes, but one of them was such a good-looking fellow – real nice and kind-looking – and only about twenty-six or seven. And he got into the last carriage, just where I was standing on the platform outside, and as soon as he got in, he put his head out of the window and made a movement to me to speak to him; and directly I went up he said quite sharp and business-like, 'Where will you be this evening at nine o'clock?' And I said, 'Here', and he said, 'All right, mind you come'. And in the evening, he came all right – only in a tweed suit and cap. Oh! he was nice – such a real gentleman and such a sweet voice. And we walked along by the river, and sat on a seat under the trees, and he had brought some lovely grapes with him for us to eat. And after that we met several evenings the same way. He was not sleeping at Tranby Croft, but at a hotel in York. And he used to leave a bunch of violets every morning for me just outside his window … and a little bit of paper twisted among the violets saying the time and place for us to meet that evening. He told me a lot about himself. He said he didn't care for the shooting and the cards and all that sort of thing, but he couldn't help himself and had to go through with it. But he did long for some real love and affection from anyone like me – only it was impossible – like in his position. He said he lived in a sort of big country house … and if ever I was in that part was to let him know.[13]

Edward too, like the young aristocrat, longed for 'some real love and affection'. He would certainly get it in abundance from a young man, by temperament loving and passionate. His ideal companion did not have to be 'especially intellectual'. He had found among Sheffield's workers men of high intelligence and considerable learning. His attraction to the self-educating George Hukin had been deepened by the intellectual affinity that sprung from their shared socialist convictions. There was little such empathy with George Merrill. He would soon discover that to argue with him was quite impossible, for any attempt to harness his thoughts in a logical form was doomed to failure. George's intelligence found its expression in a quickness of wit and a devastating repartee, but often so wide of the real mark that Edward would be left open-mouthed and unable to reply. Years later, when he quipped that George, 'never read my books', George responded: 'I am like the boy who would not eat jam because he worked where it was made'.[14] This witticism did not reflect the whole truth about George's intelligence. Edward once sent George Hukin a book, with the suggestion, 'You might hand it on to George M … as it might help him to understand what Socialism means'.[15] George told him the following year: 'I am getting on nicely with *Adam's Peak*. I like it well, its [sic] awfully interesting'.[16]

There was something refreshing in the company of the non-intellectual George and Edward came to regard his lack of education as a kind of virtue. To have grown up totally ignorant of the existence of the *Saturday Review* or the *Spectator* was a 'priceless advantage'. He had one attribute, which for the musical Carpenter must have compensated for the unbridgeable intellectual gulf between them. He had a very sweet baritone voice and 'a wonderfully good and accurate ear'. His repertoire extended from sentimental ballads and semi-comic songs to the classical English music of Purcell and Quilter. He couldn't read a note of music but mastered Shubert and Schumann *lieder*, with Edward accompanying him at the piano. Through his singing, George found his way into many hearts. Twenty years after their first meeting, Edward would reflect on the complementary nature of love; suggesting that each tends to seek and admire attributes in the other 'which he himself possesses only in a small degree', while at the same time 'some common qualities and common ground are necessary as a basis for affection'.[17]

Carpenter would quaintly describe George's large sexual appetite as an 'excess of emotionality', a kind of genius for romance and affairs of the heart. He was constantly drawn to attractive men: 'There are so many beautiful people in the world', he would say, 'people that one wants to love – and one can't love them all – I feel sometimes as if my heart would burst'. But he seemed determined to view George's sexual appetite in a kindly light: 'He could not always contain himself; and would occasionally lapse into a state full of longing, a kind of love-sickness, hysterical almost, caused either by the thought of some particular person, or by some more obscure and general cause'.[18] He came to accept George's philandering, which at the same time excused his own sexual adventures: 'Few things endear one to a partner so much as the sense that one can fully confide to him one's *affaires de coeur*. When this point of confidence has been reached, (however shocking this may sound to the orthodox) their union is permanent and assured.'[19]

Carpenter was credited with showing that 'men of Our Age

could live with a working-class lover'.[20] In 1897, he brought George to live with him at Millthorpe. It was the prospect of the imminent dissolution of his once comfortable domestic arrangements that lay behind his decision. For several years the domestic round at Millthorpe had been in the competent hands of women, but after the Adams family left, he faced the prospect of having to care for himself. George was out of work at the time, so bringing him to Millthorpe as housekeeper would also solve the problem of his periodic unemployment. He told Kate Salt:

I'm glad you approve of the plan as it stands. It's destiny, and will work out all right – even grandly – but it has been forced on me by that strange Necessity which always seems to come in and impel me to things which I have not the pluck to do of myself.[21]

At a time when concealment of sexual behaviour was a creed, George's arrival was seen as an explicit affirmation, an open display, of his homosexuality. For two men to live together unchaperoned was not just audacious, it was hazardous. George was registered as his servant, but the decision to bring him to Millthorpe was considered reckless by some of his friends and led to a flurry of letters 'kindly meant, but full of warnings and advice'.[22] Some could not understand the basis of a relationship between the highly cultivated Edward and the uneducated George. One friend suggested, rather condescendingly, that it was necessary to understand 'the great rest and refreshment that simple primitive people are to men of nervous and highly-sprung temperament'. He was much more accurate when he added that Merrill was, 'a most devoted friend and attendant', much more capable in domestic matters, Carpenter had told him, 'than any upper-class idealist would have been'.[23]

The acerbic Henry Salt was forthright: 'He was only a poor ignorant fellow from Sheffield whom Edward ought to have been able to help into decent ways; instead of which he made him a sort of magnate in the house; and was much influenced by him'.[24]

Those unaware of, or choosing to ignore the real nature of the relationship, imagined a drastic decline in Edward's domestic comfort after the long years of cossetting by the women of the Fearnehough and, later, Adams families, who had shared Millthorpe with him for several years. They conjured up visions of domestic decline; the master unfed and neglected while the promiscuous assistant amused himself elsewhere. Others, aware of just what form such 'amusements' for George might take, worried about the effect on Carpenter's standing in the locality; of his being seen to share his home with a young man who, as Carpenter freely admitted, had spent much of his early life 'in the purlieus of public-houses and in a society not too reputable'.[25]

George's faults and indiscretions were often magnified and circulated as 'grave scandals', but if Carpenter is to be believed, the country people had real affection for him and 'breathed slaughter' against his attackers. It was the 'middling' people who whispered against them, and they did not matter, 'for our lives had become necessary to each other, so that what any one said was of little importance'.[26] He didn't waver:

> I reflected that if this had been happening in a continental town, or even in a large city in England, it would have excited no attention; and that one simply had to put up with all this stir as an example of British ignorance and insularity, aggravated of course by rustic conditions.[27]

His 'faint misgivings' had more to do with whether George could settle in to life in the countryside. After having lived a sociable urban existence, would he become bored at Millthorpe and unable to endure the dullness and quiet of country life? To take him away from town life might be a great mistake, but he believed that there was much more to George, and much more in him that needed to be satisfied. A life of casual work did not enable him to express 'the *prevailing* part of his character'. He would blossom at

Millthorpe, with new experiences and, in particular, daily contact with Edward's numerous friends and visitors. On such occasions, George's wit and fun would relieve any tense or dull moments with the more serious-minded guests, although he occasionally bridled when some bright young devotee monopolised Edward.

From the day of his arrival at Millthorpe a new order began; the building of their little *ménage*, on a simple and practical basis. George turned house-keeping into an artistic pleasure for himself, soon mastering cooking, baking, and all the little minutiae of household life: 'In a wonderfully short time I found myself living in a state of comfort, both physical and mental'.[28] George took almost complete charge of their domestic life, Edward's only contribution being to dust his own study and light the fire there. The market garden business was given up and only the vegetables and fruit required to supply their needs were grown, which Edward took care of with occasional outside help.

After a visit, Edith Ellis recounted a scene of domestic harmony that said much about Carpenter's views on the division of labour between the sexes:

> One was mending his shirt, and the other a pair of socks. No incongruity struck me because Carpenter's idea of life is simplification and a real division of work. His belief is, that what a woman can do a man can always share. He has realised the truth that no occupation is a sex monopoly, but a chance for free choice, capability and division of labour. So that when Carpenter takes his share in the washing-up it seems quite as natural as when he lights a cigarette. When he neither sows nor smokes but plays Chopin, a curious realisation comes over one that there is no real difference in the arts of live music, stocking-mending or redeeming.[29]

They settled down to an orderly, very simple round of life. Edward would rise about 7 a.m. in the summer and 8 a.m. in the winter, and take a dip in the brook at the end of the garden. When it was too cold to bathe outside, he would have a wash-down in a sheltered corner of the garden. The mornings were devoted to writing, nearly always out of doors, winter or summer, in a hut that had been built for this purpose. There would be four hours of solid literary work, from time to time broken into by business matters and personal correspondence. The afternoons were free for working in the garden, receiving visitors and casual guests, or walking the surrounding wooded valleys, moors and farmlands. At 4 p.m. or so, there would be afternoon tea and at 5.00 letters would have to be got ready for the post, which went at 6.30. Supper was at 7 p.m., which was generally a more substantial meal than lunch. Sometimes tea and supper would be combined in a meal that they called 'tupper'. After supper George would usually go off to the pub, and very occasionally Carpenter would spend an hour there. He did most of his reading in the evenings, when there might also be friends to visit or entertain. He would, invariably, at some stage in the evening play the piano, especially his favourite Beethoven sonatas, with George singing *lieder* to his accompaniment. Sometimes, on a clear night he would get out his telescope and talk about the stars. Before going to bed, whatever the weather, he invariably took a walk along the lane, usually alone.

The way of life into which they settled would become habitual and would change little over the years:

> We have been practically within hail of one another all the time
> – working side by side in the garden or the house, or at most
> in adjacent rooms, meeting at nearly every meal, plunging
> together over the hills to the railway station and into Sheffield,
> or travelling in England or abroad. And I think it speaks well for
> both of us that the relation has endured this somewhat severe
> test: that it has grown indeed in grace and that our intimacy,
> though perhaps a little different in its temperamental character,
> is just as close and sincere today as it was twenty years ago.[30]

18

The Intermediate Sex

In 1906, a decade on from the Wilde scandal, the fifth edition of *Love's Coming of Age* included, for the first time, a chapter of twenty-one pages in length on the nature of the homosexual person. It was based on his *An Unknown People* pamphlet of 1897. Two years later, he published *The Intermediate Sex*.[1] Incorporating his pioneering 1894 *Homogenic Love* pamphlet. It was the first unambiguous defence of homosexuality to be published in England. It soon sold out and was reissued the following year. Subsequently, it was reprinted a further five times, the last in 1930, a year after his death.

The book *consolidated* his achievement with *Love's Coming of Age*, by now widely acknowledged as an important modernist approach to women's sexuality, even by fellow socialists. But a book on homosexuality was a much more difficult undertaking, requiring all of his literary skills. The chapter in *Love's Coming of Age* had dealt only with the homosexual's *nature*. It was not an outright defence of homosexuality or, importantly, an attack on the Labouchère clause in the 1885 Criminal Law Amendment Act. *The Intermediate Sex* was both.

The case for the repeal of the clause is boldly stated. With its imprecise offence of *gross indecency*, it had made almost any familiarity between two men the possible basis of a prosecution, throwing a shadow over even the simplest and most ordinary of endearments between males. But it was the attack on personal liberty, in extending the law's remit to the bedroom, that was most resented. It was an attempt, as Carpenter put it, 'to regulate the private and voluntary relations of adult persons to each other'.[2] It was an intrusion into the lives of homosexual men that was not applied to two persons of the opposite sex. In the interest of justice and fairness, homosexuality ought to be tolerated under exactly the same restrictions that were applied to heterosexual relationships.

A format that he used for a number of his books was to bring together material that had already been published, usually as pamphlets or journal articles. This was the case with *The Intermediate Sex*. There were four chapters: 'The Intermediate Sex', (taken unchanged from *Love's Coming of Age*); 'The Homogenic Attachment', which used parts of the *Homogenic Love* pamphlet; '*Affection in Education*' (not dealt with here), and 'The Place of the Uranian in Society', which expanded his ideas on the social functions of homosexuals, first raised in *Homogenic Love*. All the key arguments in defence of the homosexual made in these publications are brought together.

He must have decided that beginning the book with a consideration of the homosexual's *nature* would be prudent: with the defence of homosexuality as a natural variant of the sexual instinct following on. He knew that this chapter would be the most liable to render the book obscene and was best hedged around by less provocative material. Ten years on from Ellis's *Sexual Inversion*, a book, even one drawing on the substantial supportive evidence for congenital homosexuality that had accumulated over the last thirty years, was still a very risky undertaking in England.

But there was a disadvantage in opening the book with his account of the cognitive, psychological and physiological characteristics of homosexuals, as it immediately introduced the controversial idea of *sexual intermediacy*, which, as we have argued, effectively 'feminised' male and 'masculinised' female homosexuals. It was Magnus Hirschfeld who had been the most recent to claim that homosexuals were *sexuelle zwischenstufen*, combining male and female qualities and characteristics,[3] which had attracted strong criticism from male-oriented groups in Germany. Members of the 'Community of the Special' (*Gemeinschaft der Eigenen*) were the most insistent that a homosexual orientation was a cultural preference, not an inborn condition but a spiritual form of male-loving. It expressed virile masculine qualities, echoing Symonds's claim that, among the Dorians, a passion for males was considered proof of an extra-virile temperament.

As discussed earlier, in the 1850s, with the growth of forensic psychiatry, physicians were being called as expert witnesses in the prosecution of sexual crimes in large European cities, when notions such as the 'hermaphrosidy' of the paederast's mind and the effeminacy of so-called 'philopedes' became current. And a strict gender dimorphism *was* certainly being questioned when Carpenter wrote. Otto Weininger argued that all individuals combined male and female 'substance', and also described homosexuality as an 'intermediate' sexual form.[4] Charles Leland also emphasised the feminine and masculine characteristics of artistically gifted homosexual men and women,[5] and Edward Prime-Stevenson wrote of 'semisexualism'.[6]

Symonds had regarded as extraordinary the idea of homosexuals as a sex apart. He could not find in himself anything that justified the idea of a 'female soul' shut up in a male body, which he said savoured of 'bygone scholastic speculation'.[7] Similarly, Whitman's same-sex lovers were not biologically different from other men; half man, half woman. And Ellis dismissed the idea out of hand: 'It merely crystallises into an epigram the superficial impression of the matter.'[8] The issue of sexual differentiation was elusive, but he believed that the clue to homosexuality probably lay in a latent organic bisexuality; in a hermaphroditic constitution.

Carpenter asked the reader to accept that many distinctions between the sexes had by now been stripped away, making the extremes of masculinity and femininity less apparent. The reconsideration of 'femaleness' detached from a woman's procreative role had revealed 'the diversity of human temperament and character in matters relating to sex and love'. It was possible, he claimed, to identify males with a 'double temperament'; individuals in whom there was 'a balance of the feminine and masculine qualities'.[9]

Like Hirschfeld, Carpenter appealed to Ulrichs to underpin his arguments, but, we believe, misunderstood him in claiming that he had placed male homosexuals on the dividing line between the sexes'; that whilst belonging physiologically to one sex they belonged *'mentally* and *emotionally* to the other'.[10] As we have argued, for Ulrichs, what distinguished the male homosexual was not the possession of a male-female double nature but an 'inverted' *love sentiment*, that of a female towards a male. The homosexual's nature was not, as Carpenter described it, 'a balance of the feminine and masculine qualities'. Ulrichs focussed exclusively on the nature of the *sex-drive*, whilst Carpenter's 'intermediate sex' is about the possession of male and female characteristics, covering cognitive and psychological attributes and the emotions. We have seen that, when identifying a female 'love sentiment' in the male homosexual, Ulrichs did, initially, look for female bodily and behavioural markers, and assigned feminine characteristics to all male homosexuals. But with greater knowledge of the diversity of homosexual types, he had to accept that the possession of feminine qualities did not *define* the male homosexual. Only his *inverted* love sentiment marked him out. In appearance and behaviour, there were male homosexuals who were decidedly feminine but there were masculine homosexual males who did not have so-called feminine mental and physical characteristics or behavioural traits, but whose 'love sentiment' was still, feminine. Carpenter, although holding that the typical homosexual male did not exhibit pronounced femininity, nonetheless insisted that he still possessed 'the tenderer and more emotional soul-nature of a woman'.[11]

The assigning of female attributes to the male homosexual, as Hirschfeld had found, offended many men who did not care to be dubbed the 'intermediate sex' in a culture that projected a strong normative masculinity. Even after setting aside exaggerated types, the effeminate male and the butch female, Carpenter still insisted that there was 'a general tendency towards femininity of type in the male ... and towards masculinity in the female'.[12] The male tended to be 'of a rather gentle, emotional disposition', while the female was just the opposite, 'fiery, active and bold'. The mind of the male was 'generally intuitive and instinctive in its perceptions', that of the woman 'more logical, scientific and precise than usual with the normal woman'.[13]

Carpenter's views may have given homosexuals an understanding of their natures; a feeling of self-worth, and in their own way, of being *normal*. But the linking of homosexuality with femininity posed a double social stigma for a person contemplating living an openly-gay life. A very feminine youth might be pushed into a homosexual life, but a more masculine youth in appearance and behaviour, and seemingly heterosexual, would be aware of the double-stigma he faced. Even if he chose to 'come out', he would continue to have good reason to hide his homosexual preference, and even to feel ashamed. In this way, the idea of homosexuality as gender inversion 'helped to restrain the expression of homosexual identities and behaviours' and did not pose a threat to the idea of virile masculine heterosexuality that was socially-reinforced at this time. [14]

Perhaps Carpenter believed that the idea of sexual 'intermediacy' would fit with the claim that homosexuality was a congenital abnormality. Instead, it would help to reinforce the association between homosexuality and femininity. In seeking to gain acceptability in heterosexual society by dissociating themselves from femininity, many gay men tacitly supported the rigidity of gender roles and contributed to the oppression of effeminate gay men, who would bear the brunt of homophobia in the early days of gay liberation. Today, greater social recognition of the diversity of sexual tastes and practices, and the visibility of 'butch' masculine men with same-sex desires, whether gay, bisexual or just sexually adventurous, has altered public perceptions of the homosexual persona. The very feminine homosexual, the camp 'queen', endures as an object of social parody but no longer signifies a gay identity.

It is understandable that he wanted to use every plausible argument that might help the case for the recognition and acceptance of homosexuals. These essentially biological claims, however questionable, were clearly intended to counter the widespread notion that homosexuality was a psychiatric disorder, the position widely endorsed by the English medical profession at this time. Carpenter laid down a challenge to those who were 'inclined to deny to the homogenic or homosexual love, that intense, that penetrating, and at times overmastering character which would entitle it to rank as a great human passion'.[15]

After reviewing the extensive literature on homosexuality and repeating the many supportive arguments found in his previous publications, he reiterated his foremost claim, that homosexuality was 'quite instinctive and congenital', not a morbid condition. He urged the reader to accept that, step by step, on the basis of reliable evidence, this assumption was being abandoned.

If his views on the homosexual's nature may have appeared incongruous to some, and offensive to others, his claims for the recognition of the social worth of homosexuals were likely to have been more favourably received. He argued that their repression in contemporary life was a loss, and even posed a danger to social harmony. He was the first to call for homosexuals to be given equal rights with heterosexuals, and to be accepted as full members of society. Audaciously, he suggested that stable same-sex relationships should be given the 'sanction and dignity' of public recognition, anticipating the civil partnerships and marriage for same-sex couples that would come over a century later.

Homosexuals should be specially valued by society for the contributions that they made to the nation's cultural life. He doubted whether the spiritual life of the nation was ever possible without the sanction of this attachment in its institutions.

> It certainly does not seem impossible to suppose that as the ordinary love has a special function in the propagation of the race, so the other has its special function in social and heroic work and in the generation – not of bodily children – but of those children of the mind, the philosophical conceptions and ideals which transform our lives and those of society.[16]

He likened a liberated homosexual fraternity to 'a new and important' movement, which might accomplish 'the noblest work' in some distant reformed social organisation. He was aware that his call for new institutions of human solidarity might meet with opposition, certainly ridicule, but for forty years he had held true to the possibilities that Whitman had opened his eyes to. The recognition of the homosexual was not just a personal imperative, it was a part of his socialist vision.

> If the day is coming ... when Love is at last to take its rightful place as the binding and directing force of society (Instead of the

Cash-nexus), and society is to be transmuted in consequence to a higher form, then undoubtedly the superior types of Uranians – prepared for this service by long experience and devotion, as well as by much suffering – will have an important part to play in the transformation.[17]

Under the influence of the ancient Hindu text the *Bhagavad Gita*, his journey to Ceylon and India, and American Transcendentalist philosophy, he had turned against empiricism as the single path to knowledge. In particular, he could not accept that change occurred through *external* influences; by more-or-less accidental adaptation, which seemed to imply purposelessness. In reaction, he derived from the naturalist Jean-Baptiste Lamarck a theory of change through *internal* growth, which he called 'exfoliation', and which he believed would lead to the emergence of a higher form of human consciousness. This claim now surfaced in the form of sexual evolutionism:

How *far* this process may go we hardly yet know, but that it is one of the factors of future evolution we hardly doubt. I mean that the love of men towards each other – and similarly the love of women for each other – may become factors of future human evolution just as necessary and well-recognised as the ordinary loves that lead to the propagation of the race. If so, we may safely say that we see here in operation a great power which is already playing its part in moulding the world, and one which we are morally bound not to deny and disown, and not to run away from, at the risk of denying our humanity.[18]

19

—

A Brush with the Law

It was now fourteen years since he had written his first pamphlet on homosexuality. If frequently attacked for his ideas, he had escaped prosecution. But not long after the publication of *The Intermediate Sex*, a rabid anti-socialist by the name of M. D. O'Brien, a member of the England Patriotic and Anti-Socialist Association, began writing letters to Sheffield newspapers unleashing a tirade against what he called an international conspiracy of moral corruption by those who practised things which St Paul condemned as worthy of death. The less socialists said about love the better, he warned, and challenged Carpenter to a debate on the moral purity of socialism. His next move was to attend a meeting at which Carpenter was speaking on the role of the state. Choosing his moment, O'Brien asked whether state intervention ran to introducing young men to the 'vice' extolled in his writings? Carpenter countered skilfully, but by now the hall was in uproar and O'Brien was forcibly removed. He then distributed a leaflet, *Socialism and Infamy,*[1] in villages neighbouring Millthorpe. It attacked homosexuality as a vice that undermined marriage and the family. Endearments between men were 'disgusting and loathsome'; Carpenter was a moral poisoner, and George Merrill had propositioned local men.

Carpenter was holidaying in Florence with Merrill, when a concerned George Hukin sent him a copy of the pamphlet:

> He left one here. I did not see him myself, he handed it to F[annie] at the back door. A[dams] tells me he saw him, & O.B. said 'you know it's libellous. C could prosecute me. I want him to. I have just been to his house. It's empty. He's left the country and he'll never dare to come back again'.[2]

A second letter quickly followed, in which he put the blame for the crisis squarely on George:

> G is the real problem with all the stories going about concerning him. I think it would be wise to keep him away for the present. Of course one does not know how much O'Brien knows still one must be careful at present. Strange stories are afloat. Fannie told me yesterday that two different women had told her that a number of women in Dronfield were anxious to know when you were returning that they might waylay and mob you. I don't set much store by these tales although I daresay O'Brien has managed to stir up a good deal of feeling against you in that particular quarter.[3]

An apparently sanguine Carpenter did not respond to Hukin's warning until late June:

> O'Brien's explosion is really rather mad – in fact it is so extreme and violent that it overbalances itself, and will not I think carry much weight though doubtless it will damage me in places; and anyhow it is not pleasant to have him raving about up &

down the country. I do not at all think of taking any action – but in a day or two I will write a letter to the Sheffield papers – rather brief, pointing out the madness and sweeping charges in the letter against literary men, schoolteachers & everything socialistic, and inferring that little notice need be taken of it, particularly as all my views are written out in my books and can be read by everybody with much more advantage than the garbled hash which he puts forward ... Time will gloss things over; and it is perhaps a good thing that I happen to be away just now; as it makes a reason for delay.[4]

It was decided that George, who would be travelling home ahead of him, should only stay a day or two at Millthorpe, and then go away again until Edward returned, thus avoiding any meeting with O'Brien.

In letters to the *Sheffield Daily Telegraph* and the *Sheffield Independent* Carpenter appealed to readers to read his books for a true account of his ideas, and to reject O'Brien's distortions. He still had no intention of pursuing him in the courts, sharing the view of many that Oscar Wilde had precipitated his own downfall by suing the Marquess of Queensberry for libel. He was not going to walk into O'Brien's trap, but remained vulnerable. Anxious to reinforce his 'respectability' in the eyes of his neighbours, he decided to 'beat the bounds' of the parish with friends, hoping that the appearance of some of his sober upright acquaintances would favourably impress the recipients of the pamphlets. One such person was Henry Salt:

> Edward begged us to come up from Surrey, where I was then living, in order that we might accompany him in a sort of march round the parish, by way of an antidote to the slanders that had been instilled into the rustic mind. This we did, and the next day we walked in procession till there was not a farm or a cottage which had not been edified by the spectacle.[5]

O'Brien had no intention of surrendering his cause. Having failed to damage Carpenter in Sheffield, he adopted a new strategy, by writing to the Home Secretary hinting at impropriety between Carpenter and Merrill. Papers in the National Archives record that the Home Office and the Chief Constables of the Sheffield and Derbyshire constabularies all became involved and files were soon circulating between them. Although no action was taken against Carpenter, he had now been noticed by officialdom. His publications were drawn to the attention of Sir Charles Mathews, the Director of Public Prosecutions. However, Matthews judged that raising a prosecution would inevitably draw attention to Carpenter's books; posing a greater danger to public morals than leaving him alone, notwithstanding that the chapter in *The Intermediate Sex* on the 'homogenic attachment' could easily have rendered the book an 'obscene libel'. Matthews was much keener to prosecute widely circulating fictional accounts of sexual relationships. Five years later he led the prosecution against D. H. Lawrence's *The Rainbow*.

The police knew that if Carpenter was to be trapped, or at least discredited, it would be through the wayward George, and a concerted effort to find evidence of misconduct by him was made. A local farmer was persuaded to record two incidents supposedly involving indecency by Merrill. However, the allegations came to nothing and no attempt was made to prosecute Merrill. By then, as Edward delicately described it, 'under the natural consolidation of maturity', he was leading a quieter life. As for O'Brien, he later found himself in court, not to arraign Carpenter but to answer a charge of having published a pamphlet libelling his own family! It was O'Brien who ended up in prison, but the foreboding of Robert Blatchford and others on the dangers of mixing sexual reform and socialism had been justified.

20

The Fight Continued

T*he Intermediate Sex* was the highpoint of Carpenter's defence of same-sex love but issues surrounding sexuality continued to engage him. In 1902, he had published *Iolaus*, an anthology of male friendships throughout history, and went on to publish a survey of ethnological research into homosexuality among native peoples; showing the social functions, and often high status, of sexually divergent individuals, both male and female.[1] This latter study, he felt, reinforced his argument for the full participation of homosexuals in society. Two further books would include reflections on human sexuality.[2]

Two decades after he had ventured into the field of sexual politics, the time seemed right to attempt a further advance in public understanding. In 1913, the Fourteenth International Medical Congress was held in London, at which Magnus Hirschfeld was one of the principal speakers. In Germany he had been a founding member of The Scientific Humanitarian Committee, set up in 1897 to campaign for the decriminalisation of male homosexual acts that took place in private between consenting adults. Carpenter and Ellis had forged links with the group, and there had been talk of establishing an English branch or an equivalent organisation. The Congress rekindled such expectations and in July of the following year The British Society for the Study of Sex Psychology was set up, with Carpenter as its first president.

By now, he and Ellis 'stood as giants of an earlier British generation who could provide the necessary prestige to get a reform society off the ground'.[3]

The Society's main purpose was educational: to consider 'problems and questions connected with sexual psychology, from their medical, juridical and sociological aspects'. Through public meetings and published papers, it hoped to contribute to a more humane, scientifically informed, understanding of sexual questions. Although it did not have the overtly political aim of seeking a change in the law governing homosexual relationships, early on a sub-committee was set up for its study, and the Society's second pamphlet, written by Ellis, was *The Social Problem of Sexual Inversion*.

From the outset, it forged strong links with the women's movement, reinforcing the connections Carpenter had made twenty years earlier in his ground-breaking pamphlets. One of the early leading members was Stella Browne,[4] like Carpenter, a campaigner for a woman's right to make her own sexual choices. To protect itself from prosecution, the Society was cautious in its dealings, often addressing its publications specifically to members of the educational, legal and medical professions. The law against obscene publications that had snared Ellis's book remained in place, as witnessed by the prosecution of. *The Rainbow*, and much later, the prosecution of Lawrence's Lady *Chatterley's Lover* in 1960. Support for the Society was strong among progressives and it helped to raise awareness and understanding of homosexuality, but it is unlikely that it 'changed public opinion in any significant way or influenced government policy'.[5] In 1920, the cumbersome name of the Society was changed to The British Sexological Society.

In the intervening years leading up to the Second World War, homosexual offences were dealt with harshly, mainly under the 1885 Act. During the war, with an influx of American servicemen, sexual restraint seems to have been abandoned and the servicemen's needs were met as much by men as by women. But after the war there was concerted police crack-down. Pretty young constables were used as *agent provocateurs* to entrap homosexuals, which led to a large increase in arrests and prosecutions for soliciting for immoral purposes or for acts of gross indecency. Confessions extracted under duress, inducements to turn crown witness, and the searching of properties without warrants, seemed standard police practice when dealing with homosexuals; often overlooked by judges and jury's intent on upholding the integrity of the police. Homosexuals were fair game. In March 1955, two off-duty police constables from the Metropolitan Police were found guilty of blackmailing a commercial traveller and received jail sentences of two years. It was a warning:

> Had it been conceivable to produce a gay man's survival guide at that time it would have urged him never to reveal his name or address, never to discuss how he earned his living or where he worked, never to take anybody to his home or give anybody his telephone number and never to write letters, whether affectionate or not, to anybody with whom he was sexually involved or even to anybody he knew to be gay.[6]

By the 1950s, 'much of the business of the criminal calendar was sexual', and much of it concerned homosexuality.[7]

The hostile attitude towards gay men intensified, leading to a succession of major scandals involving prominent individuals. In 1951, Guy Burgess and Donald Maclean, both homosexual and impeccable members of the British establishment, defected to the Soviet Union. The threat that homosexuals were seen to pose for public order and decency was now elevated to the threat they posed to the security of the state. In 1955, John Vassall, a homosexual serving as a clerk in the British Embassy in Moscow, was entrapped by the KGB and recruited as a spy. He was actively involved in espionage until his exposure in 1962.

Other prominent individuals were being ensnared. In 1952, Alan Turing, the mathematician and computer scientist who helped to crack war-time German signal codes, was prosecuted for 'gross indecency'. As an alternative to a prison sentence, he agreed to be chemically castrated, a clear echo of Ellis's observations on who was most fit, or unfit, to 'carry on the race'. The conviction destroyed Turing, who died two years later from cyanide poisoning, which an inquest determined was suicide. In October 1953, the celebrated actor Sir John Gielgud, like many gay men, usually highly discreet when seeking casual sex, was arrested and convicted for 'cruising' in a public lavatory. The acting fraternity closed ranks and Guilgud's disgrace did not end his career, although there were calls for him to surrender his knighthood, and he suffered a nervous break-down some months later. Tom Driberg, the *Daily Express*'s gossip columnist 'William Hickey' in the 1940s, had benefited from the protection of a powerful press baron and his connections with the police to escape charges when caught soliciting in public toilets. He never made any secret of his homosexuality and continued 'cruising' after he became a Labour Member of Parliament.

A large number of much less prominent individuals were now being prosecuted for various homosexual offences. The activities of schoolmasters, scoutmasters, youth leaders and clergymen were of particular interest to zealous police forces. Salacious cases involving individuals well-known in their communities were reported in the popular national newspapers, although less so in 'family-centred' local ones. In 1954, in Barnsley, police went to extraordinary lengths to find evidence to prosecute thirteen individuals, predominantly working-class men, accused of homosexual offences with a single individual. This, and other trials involving group sex, opened people's eyes to the prevalence of homosexuality outside of the major cities, and also scotched the idea that homosexuality was purely an upper-class vice.[8]

The year 1954 was remarkable, for in no year before or after were so many trials for homosexual offences reported in the press. That year saw the prosecution, of three prominent men: Lord Montague of Beaulieu, his first-cousin Michael Pitt-Rivers, and Peter Wildeblood, the diplomatic correspondent of the *Daily Mail*. The trial made Montague the most notorious public figure of his generation. He had already been acquitted the previous year of serious sexual offences against two boy scouts. Frustrated by Montague's escape, the police had a stroke of luck after a homosexual network was uncovered among RAF airmen serving in Korea. Letters discovered by the RAF police linking two airmen with Lord Montague were passed to the Metropolitan police, who promised the airmen immunity if they turned Queen's evidence and the whole trial rested on their testimonies. In addition to a number of homosexual offences, the three were also charged with 'conspiring' to commit the offences. This was unusual in such cases, but indicated the prosecution's determination to obtain convictions. All three men were found guilty on all offences and imprisoned. As with Wilde, the incongruity of class differences helped to convict the men, who could offer no plausible explanation for their association with two working-class individuals. This, and numerous other trials during this period, have been described by Jeffrey Weeks as attempts to stereotype male homosexuals 'as decadent, corrupt, effete and effeminate'.[9] Furthermore, when the World Health Organisation was established in 1948, homosexuality was classified as a 'psychiatric disorder' and could be authoritatively described as 'a severe mental sickness requiring psychotherapy'.[10]

Following his imprisonment, Wildeblood published *Against the Law*.[11] It was an early 'coming out' story, but also a powerful argument for homosexual law reform and the reform of prisons; bringing to light the appalling conditions that he had experienced in HMP Wormwood Scrubs. He later wrote A *Way of Life*,[12] essays describing the lives of individuals living with and accepting their homosexuality, which may have helped to 'normalise' it in some people's eyes. But, by the end of 1954, there were over a thousand men in prison for homosexual offences.

The post-war years had seen government departmental committees set up to examine issues of public concern, in particular, capital punishment, marriage, divorce, and gambling. The convictions of Montague and his friends led to questions in high places and support for some measure of homosexual law reform became a topic of public discussion. A leader in the *Sunday Times* on 28 March 1954, 'Law and Hypocrisy' supported a review of the existing law, and there were calls for action from members of both the House of Lords and the Commons. The homophobic Home Secretary, Sir David Maxwell-Fife, who played no small part in the drive to prosecute more gay men, bowed to pressure and in August set up a Home Office departmental committee to examine and report on the state of the law relating to homosexual offences *and* prostitution. The bringing together of two dissimilar topics within a single enquiry was confusing, but it enabled the popular press to describe the eventual findings of the committee as the 'Vice Report'. Meanwhile the police remained busy. In July, in Birmingham, twenty-eight men were given prison sentences for isolated homosexual incidents stretching back a number of years. The origin of the prosecutions was the 'discovery' by the police of the diary of one of the men. The investigation and trials consumed an inordinate amount of police and judicial time.

Sir John Wolfenden, then Vice-Chancellor of Reading University, was chosen to chair the committee. Unbeknown to the government, two years earlier Wolfenden's then eighteen-year-old son Jeremy had told him that he was homosexual. This was never revealed during the enquiry but it caused Wolfenden considerable anxiety, as he was aware that his son was leading a promiscuous life. According to his biographer, his father wrote to him at the time asking him to 'stay out of his way' and to 'wear rather less makeup'.[13]

In 2007, to mark the fortieth anniversary of the passing of the 1967 Sexual Offences Act decriminalising gay sex in private, the BBC commissioned the film *Consenting Adults*, which in part dramatised the strained relationship between father and son. If the father became famous, the son became infamous. Recruited by M15, before becoming *The Daily Telegraph*'s foreign correspondent in Moscow, he was caught by the KGB having sex with a man. Allegedly he was subsequently blackmailed by both M15 and the KGB. His father would go on to be ranked forty-ninth in the *Pink Paper*'s 1997 list of 500 lesbian and gay heroes!

The committee was made up of eleven men and four women. The legal profession was well-represented by a High Court judge, a former Scottish procurator fiscal, a solicitor and two magistrates; the clergy by an Anglo-Catholic priest and a Presbyterian minister; the medical profession by a psychiatrist and a general practitioner; politics by a Conservative Party peer, who was also a Foreign Office minister, and a Labour and a Conservative Member of Parliament. There was also a university head and the chairwoman of the Scottish Association of Girls' Clubs. There was an echo of Carpenter's 'impure hush' when the committee decided that throughout the inquiry, for the sake, it appears, of the women members, homosexuals should be referred to as 'Huntleys' and prostitutes as 'Palmers' (after the biscuit manufacturer).

The committee first met in September 1954 and sat for sixty-two days, of which thirty-two were used to interview witnesses. Clearly, it needed to hear the life-experiences of homosexuals (not surprisingly, it did not interview any prostitutes), and it discussed how this could be achieved. The idea of placing advertisements in newspapers and magazines was soon abandoned. Instead, it decided only to interview three homosexual men: the convicted Peter Wildeblood; Carl Winter, director of the Fitzwilliam Museum in Cambridge, who gave his evidence as 'Mr White'; and Patrick Trevor-Roper, a distinguished eye surgeon and brother of the historian Hugh Trevor-Roper, who was 'the Doctor'. It seems that these were the only men who could be found to appear as openly gay witnesses.

The philosophical basis of the Committee's deliberations was John Stuart Mill's principle, laid down in 1859 in his book *On Liberty*, that it was not the function of the law to interfere with purely *self-regarding* actions; in this case, sexual behaviour between consenting adults in private, even though such behaviour would certainly be considered by many to be both socially undesirable, and immoral. The purpose of the law, in such cases, was to preserve public order and decency, to protect the citizen from what was offensive or injurious, and to provide sufficient safeguards against the exploitation and corruption of others. It was not its function to intervene in the private lives of citizens, or to seek to enforce any particular pattern of sexual behaviour. The committee therefore made the recommendation, supported by a majority of its members, that homosexual behaviour in private, if between two consenting adults over the age of twenty-one, should no longer be a prosecutable offence. As it was clumsily worded in the report: '[U]nless a deliberate attempt be made by society through the agency of the law to equate the sphere of crime with that of sin, there must remain a realm of privacy that is in brief, not the law's business'.

The public debate that followed the committee's recommendation would include a famous exchange of views between Lord Denning, a leading English judge, and H. L. A. Hart, a prominent jurisprudential scholar. Denning rejected the committee's reliance on Mill's principle, holding that 'popular' morality should be allowed to influence law-making. Even private acts should be subject to legal sanction if they were held to be morally unacceptable by the 'reasonable' man, in order to preserve the moral fabric of society. Hart accepted Mill's principle as the foundation for the committee's recommendation, highlighting a clash between two jurisprudential theories, that of 'legal moralism' and 'legal liberalism'.

In addition to the three gay men whose lives had been affected by the law, evidence was given by police, probation officers, psychiatrists and religious leaders. The attitudes towards homosexuality were overwhelmingly condemnatory, the majority opposing any change to the existing law. A number of medical and psychiatric witnesses maintained the position that homosexuality was a 'disorder'. Trevor-Roper vigorously challenged this assertion, telling the committee that most gay men led normal and well-adjusted lives and posed no threat to public order, or to children. The existing law did nothing but encourage the blackmailer, whilst many young gay men had taken, or attempted to take, their own lives because of isolation or depression brought on by homophobia. On this issue, the committee would eventually conclude that homosexuality could not legitimately be regarded as a disease. The three witnesses had manifestly demonstrated that homosexuality was compatible with full mental and physical health.

Although the committee rejected the view that homosexuality was a sickness, it did not (probably dared not) argue that it was neither sinful nor immoral. Its recommendations were essentially practical and pragmatic, Wolfenden hoping that it would satisfy both reformists and moralists. The report emphasised that the committee was recommending only 'a limited modification of the law', and that it should not be seen as indicating that the law could be indifferent to other forms of homosexual behaviour. It was not a 'general licence' for homosexuals to act as they pleased.

One member of the committee, James Adair, the former Procurator Fiscal for Glasgow, was recalcitrant throughout the hearings; constantly seeking to undermine, often with lurid representations of homosexual life, the liberal report that he saw emerging. After its publication, he embarked on a minor campaign for the moralists, by promoting his own 'minority' report.

Other recommendations by the committee included: reviews of the maximum sentences for buggery, gross indecency and indecent assault, male prostitution and importuning for immoral purposes. There were also recommendations on the organisation of approved schools, prison medical services and the treatment of homosexual offenders. The committee's purely legalistic approach was a missed opportunity, as the historian Patrick Higgins has written: 'Without doubt its chief weakness was its failure to understand or appreciate (except in the most negative terms) the importance of the homosexual subculture. The committee had a number of glimpses into this world but, as with so much associated with the 'distasteful problem' of homosexuality, it preferred to keep its distance'.[14] The report was published on 5 September 1957.

Much of the popular press was outraged by its key recommendation but as Antony Grey wrote: 'it gave a tremendous fillip to those of us who scented an anticipatory whiff of victory in our overdue quest for justice'.[15] There are only two brief passing references to Carpenter in Grey's book. Although, as Jeffrey Weeks has written, in the arguments of the reformers there was 'little evocation of pioneering names',[16] many of Grey's arguments in defence of the homosexual could have been taken straight out of *The Intermediate Sex*:

> Those of us who are homosexual or bisexual are entitled, as much as any other members of society, to our basic rights and equalities as citizens; to our human dignity; to the freedom to

be what we are; to equal opportunities with everyone else to live our lives fully and openly, forming and sustaining whatever personal, domestic and social relationships we choose, without official or unofficial pressure to desist, dissemble or conform.[17]

His book tells the inside story of the drawn-out battle for the reform advocated by Wolfenden, and the subsequent course of the developing movement for gay rights.

Soon after the publication of the report, the Home Secretary agreed to see a delegation from the newly-established Homosexual Law Reform Society, but it became clear that the government intended to legislate on prostitution, but not on the homosexual part of the report. True to its word, in 1959 it passed The Street Offences Act, which included a provision against females loitering for the purpose of prostitution. This law was widely employed by the police, who continued to act as if the Wolfenden Report did not exist, to arrest homosexuals for importuning. At least two members of the committee had wanted to include a severe criticism of the police for using *agents provocateurs*, but were side-lined. The police were exonerated: 'It must, in our view, be accepted that a police officer legitimately resorts to a degree of subterfuge in the course of his duty', the report stated. In December 1958, two middle-aged men living together in Middlesbrough will be closely questioned by police about alleged homosexual offences. Soon after, they will gas themselves, leaving a poignant note asking to be buried together.

On 7 March 1958, a powerful letter in support of Wolfenden's principal legislative proposal appeared in *The Times*, signed by thirty-four distinguished individuals, among them Clement Attlee, Bertrand Russell, A. J. Ayer, Isaiah Berlin, J. B. Priestley, Stephen Spender, Julien Huxley, Bishop Trevor Huddleston and the bishops of Oxford and Birmingham. The decades-long debate on homosexuality within the Church of England was set in train when the signatories to an opposing letter to *The Times*, arguing that such legislation would divide the nation and 'bring a most unsavoury subject into undesirable prominence', included the bishops of Carlisle and Rochester.

A month after the letter to *The Times*, a small number of individuals in favour of reform, including signatories to the letter, not all homosexual, came together to establish the Homosexual Law Reform Society. In the same month The Albany Trust, a charity complementing the HLRS was set up to promote psychological health in homosexual men. In time, the Trust would develop into a pioneering counselling organisation for gay men, lesbians and other sexual minorities. In May 1960, over 1000 people attended the first public meeting of HLRS. Antony Grey became acting secretary in 1962 and full secretary the following year. In 1970 it would change its name to the Sexual Law Reform Society, in order to campaign more widely for the rights of sexual minorities.

Resistance to reforming the law persisted and there was little movement until 1965, when Humphry Berkeley, a Conservative MP, introduced a private members' bill to have the law changed in line with the Wolfenden recommendation. He was supported by Lord Aaron, a Conservative peer, and Leo Abse, a Labour Member of Parliament. They were encouraged by an opinion poll that year, commissioned by the *Daily Mail*, which had found that 63 percent of respondents did not think that homosexuality should be a crime, with 36 percent saying that it should. But the view that homosexuality was an illness persisted, being shared by 93 percent of respondents, who believed that homosexual men 'were in need of medical or psychiatric treatment'.

Berkeley's bill passed its second reading in the House of Commons, by 164 to 107 votes, but its passage was interrupted by the dissolution of Parliament for a general election. The Conservative government had been rocked by a series of scandals, and latterly by the case of John Profumo, who when Secretary of State for War, was found to be having a liaison with a prostitute who had been associating with a member of the Russian Embassy in London. This precipitated the resignation of the Prime Minister, Harold Macmillan, who was succeeded for a short period by the Earl of Home. Labour, now led by Harold Wilson, won the election, but with a majority of only four seats he faced legislative difficulties. Hoping to strengthen his government, he called a snap election in March 1966, increasing his majority to ninety-six and bringing into the Commons more MPs sympathetic to a change in the law on homosexuality. Taking full advantage of its large majority, Labour became a reforming and liberalising government during its six years in office; introducing a number of new laws in response to public campaigns on abortion, divorce, capital punishment and theatre censorship.

Berkeley lost his seat at the 1966 election and the resurrected Bill was steered through the Commons by Leo Abse. Although many members, of both Houses, did not condone homosexuality, it was felt that the law should not be used to punish sexual behaviour in private. The Bill had now cut through party ranks, with both major parties permitting a *conscience* vote on the legislation. To the surprise of some, it was also supported by senior members of the Church of England, including Michael Ramsey, the Archbishop of Canterbury. Ramsey believed that homosexual acts were always wrong, but the case for altering the law in respect of consenting adults in private rested on reason and justice.

Having passed all stages in the Commons, after a final intense all-night debate, the Lords passed the Bill without a division, and the Sexual Offences Act received the Royal Assent on 27 July 1967. It made consensual sex in private between two men over the age of twenty-one, five years higher than the then age of heterosexual consent, no longer an indictable offence. (It did not apply to the Merchant Navy or to the armed forces). The privacy restriction meant that while two men could have sex together, a third person could not be present, which led to many prosecutions of individuals engaged in group sex.

The Act did not come into effect in Scotland until 1981, following legislation the previous year. The province of Northern Ireland posed a particular problem because of the overwhelming antagonism against homosexuality in the Protestant community. In 1978, the government tried to have it enacted there through an Order in Council, but it was opposed by the twelve Ulster MPs, urged on by a 'Save Ulster from Sodomy' campaign led by the Reverend Ian Paisley. Following a successful sexual discrimination case brought in the European Court of Human Rights in 1981, it was put into effect in the province in 1982 through an Order in Council.

Although a Labour government had passed the legislation, the hostility that Carpenter had experienced by mixing sex and socialism persisted. After the passing of the Act, Richard Crossman, then Leader of the House of Commons, reflected in his diary:

> Frankly it's an unpleasant Bill and I myself don't like it. It may be twenty years ahead of public opinion; certainly, working-class people jeer at their Members at the weekend and ask them why they're looking after the buggers at Westminster instead of looking after the unemployed at home. It has gone down very badly that the Labour party should be associated with such a Bill.[18]

And the subject continued to be problematic for the party. In 1981 it published a discussion paper, *The Rights of Gay Men and Women*, which was a clear restatement of Carpenter's position: 'As socialists we cannot be concerned about inequalities of class, wealth and privilege and ignore the inequalities experienced by minorities such as homosexuals. The elimination of prejudice and injustice in our society is fundamental to the fight for socialism'. After being attacked by a homophobic right-wing press, the paper was 'quickly buried, never to be seen again'.[19]

Although of historical importance, the passing of the Act, with its limited scope, was not a moment of sudden liberation for gay men. Lord Arran, who had done so much to promote the change in the law, afterwards asked that gay people should show their thanks 'by comporting themselves quietly and with dignity ... any form of ostentatious behaviour now or in the future would be utterly distasteful, leading to the sponsors of the bill regretting what they had done'.[20] But in the following decade the prosecution of homosexual offences not protected by the new law trebled. The effect of legal prohibition upon individuals' sexual behaviour, as Wolfenden had recognised, would not deter them from engaging in mutually-desired conduct of a private and personal nature.

The 1967 Act was seen by many as only a first, and limited, step. In 1969, the Committee for Homosexual Equality was established, to further promote legal and social equality in England and Wales for gay men, lesbians and bisexuals. (It had begun life in Manchester in 1964 as the North Western Homosexual Law Reform Committee.) CHE was active in the 1970s, after changing its name to the Campaign for Homosexual Equality, with the aim of becoming a national campaigning body for England and Wales. Its members spear-headed the first London Pride march, held on 1 July 1972; a date chosen as the nearest Saturday to the anniversary of the Stonewall riots. A new group, London Friend, was also set up that year to provide counselling, much like the earlier Albany Trust. There was a need for its services, as in the 70s a large number of young men between the ages of sixteen and twenty-one were being prosecuted for consensual homosexual acts; making the age of consent a continuing campaigning objective of reform groups. By now, the issue of discrimination against sexual minorities had crossed party lines. In 1975 a Conservative Group for

Homosexual Equality (TORCHE) was set up to lobby within the Tory Party.

The ardent reformers had fought hard to achieve their objectives but their role should not be overstated. The open support that came from a sizeable number of individuals who were not homosexual was critical, and ultimately helped to force through the change in the law. And there were, argues Jeffrey Weeks, significant cultural changes at work that influenced thinking about sexual relationships. Reform came about because 'it was finally seen that the contradictions in the social position of male homosexuals was absurd'. Their 'inherent instability' was incompatible with the more relaxed social climate of post-war 'affluent' Britain; a part of the long post-war boom in capitalist society. The 1967 Act was a 'fissure in the walls', a 'narrow and limited achievement'. But this fissure was one through which the more radical forces that appeared after its passing would force their way. The reformers had wrought 'more than they thought – or sometimes cared for'.[21]

In 1970, a more radical phase had opened with the first meeting of the UK Gay Liberation Front, inspired by the movement in the USA that sprung up following the Stonewall riots. Its founding marked a significant shift in gay sensibility and perspectives. CHE was focussing its efforts on lobbying the government for specific legal reforms, while the GLF was an activist organisation seeking a wider social acceptance of lesbian and gay men and their culture. It set out to be noticed and gained considerable media attention, and some notoriety, through various high-profile direct-action activities, such as street theatre, 'gay days', and sit-ins. The most outrageous was when members disrupted a meeting of the Festival of Light, a short-lived grassroots organisation formed by Christians to challenge the 'permissive' society. It was fair game for GLF members, who stormed the meeting, released mice into the hall, unfurled banners, staged a 'kiss in', and performed other provocative stunts, before succeeding in gaining access to the basement of the hall and plunging the meeting into darkness.

The GLF was dynamic, but inherently unstable, with conflicting ideologies and priorities being advocated by its members. These internal disputes did, however, lead to some positive spin-offs – Gay Switchboard, *Gay News* and Icebreakers, for example. During the 70s and 80s a diverse assortment of campaigning groups also emerged: Outrage, the Lesbian and Gay Alliance, Dykes and Fagots Together, and Lesbian Avengers, to name the most visible. These groupings would all, if asked, proclaim, 'we are here, we are proud, and we are not going away'.

Negative attitudes towards homosexuality were strongly influenced by the HIV/Aids pandemic that erupted in the 80s, and which became identified almost exclusively with gay and bisexual men. This stigma resulted in higher levels of sexual prejudice: in 1987 the British Social Attitudes Survey reported that 70 percent of those questioned believed that homosexuality 'was always or mostly wrong'. The following year, the subject of sex-education in schools became an explosive issue, after the Conservative government introduced a Local Government Act, in which Clause 28 prohibited local authorities from 'promoting' homosexuality, either by publishing teaching materials or approving its teaching in their schools. It became a highly divisive issue, forcing lesbian, gay and bisexual student-support groups in schools and colleges to close, for fear of breaking the law. Clause 28 galvanised the GLBT community, but organisations not associated with gay rights, such as The Family Planning Association, also sought its removal. It was not repealed until 2000, when it was one of the first pieces of legislation enacted by the newly established Scottish Assembly. England and Wales had to wait until 2003 for the removal of the clause.

In *The Intermediate Sex*, Carpenter had called for homosexuals to be given 'their fitting place and sphere of usefulness in the general scheme of society'.[22] The spate of legislation that followed the 1967 Act more than fulfilled his wish. In 1994, in England, Wales, Scotland and Northern Ireland, the age of consent was reduced to eighteen. In 2000, it was further reduced to sixteen (2001 in Northern Ireland), bringing it into line with the age of heterosexual consent.

Two-thousand-and-five was a landmark year: civil partnerships were legalised for same-sex couples, and individuals were able to apply to change their gender identity. In the same year, in England and Wales, same-sex couples were given the right to adopt children. This was extended to Scotland in 2009 and to Northern Ireland in 2013.

The 2010 Equality Act included clauses giving protections on sexual orientation and gender identity. In 2014, same-sex marriage was legalised in England, Wales and Scotland, and in Northern Ireland in 2020. In 2016, the ban on LGBT individuals serving openly in the armed forces was lifted, and the services began to actively seek to recruit LGBT persons. The Royal Navy now allows gay sailors to hold civil partnership ceremonies aboard ship, and all the services allow personnel to participate in Gay Pride marches wearing full uniform.

Two-thousand-and-seventeen (2018 in Scotland and Northern Ireland) saw the last act in the history of gay oppression, when individuals who had been cautioned or convicted under laws since abolished were given an automatic pardon. It has become known informally as the Alan Turing law, a posthumous tribute to the tragic loss of a very remarkable man.

These changes in the legal status of homosexuals and other sexual minorities have been reflected in significant shifts in public attitudes towards same-sex relationships. In contrast to the 1987 survey, in which 70 percent of those questioned believed that homosexuality 'was always or mostly wrong', a poll conducted in 2017 by the Office for National Statistics found that 86 percent of respondents believed that homosexuality should be accepted by society. And a Pew Research Centre poll in 2019 found that

77 percent of respondents supported same-sex marriage. All those years ago, when contrasting homosexual unions with the 'ordinary marriage', Carpenter had written:

> It would seem high time, I say, that public opinion should recognise these facts; and so, give to this attachment the sanction and dignity which arises from public recognition. It is often said how necessary for the morality of the ordinary marriage is some public recognition of the relation and some accepted standard of conduct in it. May not, to a lesser degree, something of the same kind be true of the homogenic attachment? It has had its place as a recognised and guarded institution in the elder and more primitive societies; and it seems quite probable that a similar place will be accorded it in the societies of the future.[23]

21

Remembering

In 1914, on his seventieth birthday, Carpenter received a commendatory address carrying the signatures, one for each year of his life, of world-wide prominent writers, politicians and other public figures. When his autobiography appeared two years later, *The Times* greeted it as the life of 'one of the most significant and interesting figures of a transitional time'. To a reviewer in the *Athenaeum*, he was always 'the loveably sympathetic and serious humanist'. There were numerous tributes on his eightieth birthday, including one carrying the signatures of all members of the Labour government cabinet, led by Ramsay MacDonald. Decades earlier, MacDonald was a youthful member of the Bristol Socialist Society when Carpenter gave it five pounds, which was used to establish a library. MacDonald became the librarian, making the selection of books, and, of course, reading them. He never forgot Carpenter's contribution to his education. 'The good-will of few others is so pleasing to me … in the evenings I often think of you', he wrote.[1] Carpenter died five years later, still revered in the Labour movement.

He had also left an indelible impression among young men struggling with their homosexuality; fighting self-repression, fearing ostracism, exposure or blackmail, and leading unhappy secretive lives. Those who had sought to fathom the subterranean messages of love between men in *Towards Democracy*, found in *The Intermediate Sex* a life-enhancing exposition of the nature of homosexual love, and its defence. He was seen as an exemplar; a man courageously living out his innermost beliefs. A father figure, even in his sixties youthful in body and mind, some much younger men, with whom he was often tantalising flirtatious, found him sexually alluring.

Walter Seward, whose letters reveal that he shared more than a close friendship with him, had written: 'if you only knew the relief it is to unpack oneself after years of repression ... you've opened the gates for me & I know you won't slam them in my face when I am coming to my own at last'.[2] Harry Bishop, who, in explicit language, shared with Carpenter his sexual adventures in London, had told him: 'You don't know, dear Carpenter, how often I long to see you. With you there are topics I can talk about which I do not care to talk about with anyone else in the world'.[3] Five individuals born before or soon after 1895 would speak in their old age of how enlightening and consoling his books had been in helping them to accept their homosexuality.[4] And there were young homosexual working-class men who he had taken under his wing, not without a touch of romance, and helped them to educate themselves. At his prompting, George Clemas, a serving soldier, had been reading Plato's *Phaedrus* and was looking forward to discussing it with him. Writing to 'ever-dear Clem', and his fellow soldier and lover Joe, he was sending them a copy of *Adam's Peak to Elephanta*, 'with all best wishes, dear boy, for your birthday. Be kind to the book! I think you will enjoy reading it, and I want you specially to linger over the four chapters VIII to XI, entitled A Visit to the Gnãani ... but you – both you and Joe – will like the travel part – how jolly it would be to go again on such a journey. I should enjoy it, and feel now as if I could walk all over Adam's Peak again!'[5]

For some friends, in his old age he had slipped into obscurity as the force of his personality was no longer felt. On hearing of his passing, Bernard Shaw, with whom in heady days he had played piano duets, told a mutual friend: 'I found it difficult to realise that he was not still here'.[6] And Morgan Forster recorded: 'Astonishing how he drains away'.[7] But his striking physical appearance, the sound of his voice, the radiance of his personality were not easily lost on those whom he had touched most closely. He had startled many with his beauty. Henry Salt, meeting him for the first time, was 'struck by his most wonderful eyes … I used to think sometimes that he tried to withdraw and, so to speak, to sheath their almost piercing brilliance, out of consideration for some lack-lustre companion like myself'.[8] The publisher Edward Dent never met him without being 'enthralled by his beauty of person and beauty of voice'.[9]

Shortly after his death, those who knew him best expressed their thoughts on a man who, for Salt, was 'one of the most remarkable men of his time'. What distinguished him was *seership*, 'serene and illuminative wisdom'.[10] For Laurence Housman (brother of the poet A. E. Housman) he was, 'a brave man and a brave writer, and the outspokenness of the present age on things that were "unmentionable" a generation ago is very largely due to his life and influence, and to the moral courage which the beauty of his own life and character inspired in others'.[11]

On the anniversary of his birth, Forster gave a BBC talk.[12] He was concerned to draw the right picture of the man and discussed what he should say with one of Carpenter's literary executors. It did not seem to bode well for their friend: 'Unless Labour is brought in, the centenary will be a small affair; you and I and a few others, value E. for his teaching and example about personal relations, but this won't cut enough ice; most people remember him as a social prophet and reformer and worker in the Labour movement'.[13] Although it was Carpenter's teaching and example about personal relations that had driven Forster's own creative life, before the microphone, he did not say so. The closest he came to revealing why Carpenter had had a lasting influence was when he remarked that, for him, love was 'the final earthly reality'. And, possibly fearing complicity, he did not tell the truth about Carpenter's earthly love and his brave stand for gay equality.

After a lifetime of dissimulation about his own sexuality, Forster could not bring himself to talk about Carpenter's gay life. Twenty-seven years later he was to make amends for not giving him his due, with the publication of his novel *Maurice;* which was also an act of posthumous truth-telling about his own sexuality. It was Carpenter's belief in homosexual love that had attracted Forster in his loneliness. While imbibing the atmosphere of Millthorpe, a playful pinch on his behind by the flirtatious George Merrill released the spurt of creative energy that produced the homosexual-themed *Maurice.*

The novel was as much about the cruelty of class barriers as about intolerance of homosexuality: 'The feeling that can impel a gentleman towards a man of lower class stands self-condemned', Forster had the upper-class Maurice say before he was seduced by the working-class Alec. Forster was determined that, in his fictional world, two men, of whatever class, should fall in love and remain in it 'for the ever and ever', although they would have to live outside family and class.

Carpenter was one of a small number of friends who read the manuscript, telling Forster that he was delighted that the story had ended 'on a major chord'. He was afraid that, at the last, Forster was going to let Alec go, 'but you saved him & saved the story'. The end, if improbable, was not impossible, and was 'the one bit of real romance – wh [*sic*] those who understand will love'.[14]

By the time he wrote *Maurice,* Forster had accepted that he loved men and could no longer continue to renounce his desire for physical gratification. In November 1915, a year after finishing the novel, unable to enlist, he went to Alexandria as a Red Cross searcher, interviewing the wounded for information about missing soldiers. Sexually tormented, he unburdened himself to Carpenter:

> Dear Edward, you continue the greatest comfort. I don't want to grouse, as so much is all right with me, but this physical loneliness has gone on for too many months, and with it springs and grows a wretched fastidiousness, so that even if the opportunity for which I yearn offered, I fear I might refuse it. In such a refusal there is nothing spiritual – it is rather a sign that the spirit is being broken. I am sure that some of the decent people I see daily would be willing to save me if they knew, but they don't know, can't know ... I sit leaning over them for a bit and there it ends – except for images that burn into my sleep; I know that though you have heard this and sadder cases 1000 times before, you will yet be sympathetic, and that is why you are such a comfort to me. It's awful to live with an unsatisfied craving, now and then smothering it but never killing it or even wanting to. If I could get one solid night it would be something.[15]

Carpenter had blazed a trail that had liberated Forster and others; disentangled sexuality from artificial codes and provided the normative counterpart to D. H. Lawrence's resolve to make the sex relation precious instead of shameful. He had nurtured the emotionally responsive, sexually liberated Edwardians, particularly some of the Bloomsbury set, who gave voice to the 'religion of the heart'. Forster understood, more than others, that the love that Carpenter most cared about had a defining figuration in many personal histories, and that his own life was one into which a part of Carpenter was permanently woven. The man presented by him as unlikely to have much earthly immortality had taught him truths that he had absorbed, and which had impelled his artistic life; supreme truths, above all, the primacy of personal relationships and the imperiousness of the body's commands. Close to death, Carpenter knew what form his earthly immortality would take: 'I know we have done our work, even if not a soul remembers us. We live in their limbs, in their eyes and in their laughter'.[16]

Bibliography

Manuscript Collections

Sheffield City Council, Libraries Archives and Information. Sheffield Archives: The Edward Carpenter Collection. (CC)

The Harry Ransom Centre, University of Texas: The Havelock Ellis Collection. (HRC)

The University of Bristol Special Collections: The John Addington Symonds Collection. (UBSC)

The London Library: Manuscript of Symonds's memoirs. (LL)

I am grateful for permissions to consult and use material from these collections.

Letters

Letters from, and to, Carpenter: The Edward Carpenter Collection (CC).

Ellis's, Symonds's, and Carpenter's Letters: The Harry Ransom Centre, University of Texas. (HRC)

The Letters of John Addington Symonds, 3 vols., edited by Herbert M. Schueller and Robert L. Peters, Wayne State University Press, 1967–9.

The Letters of Olive Schreiner and Havelock Ellis, edited by Y. C. Drazin, Peter Lang, 1992.

The Letters of Olive Schreiner, edited by S. C. Cronwright-Schreiner, Fisher Unwin, 1924.

Olive Schreiner Letters, edited by Richard Rive, Oxford Clarendon Press, 1988.

Works Cited

Edward Carpenter
Towards Democracy (1883)
England's Ideal (1887)
Civilisation: Its Cause and Cure (1889)
Homogenic Love and its Place in a Free Society (1894)
Love's Coming of Age (1896)
An Unknown People (1897)
From Adam's Peak to Elephanta (1902)
Iolaus: An Anthology of Friendship (1902)
The Art of Creation (1904)
Days with Walt Whitman (1906)
The Intermediate Sex (1908)
The Drama of Love and Death (1912)
Intermediate Types among Primitive Folk (1914)
My Days and Dreams (1916)
Pagan and Christian Creeds (1920)

John Addington Symonds
A Problem in Greek Ethics (1883)
A Problem in Modern Ethics (1891)
Memoirs (1892)

Havelock Ellis
The New Spirit (1890)
Sexual Inversion (1896 and 1897)
The Task of Social Hygiene (1912)
The Individual and the Race (1939)
My Life (1940)

Secondary Sources

Ackerley, J. R. (Joe Randolph). *My Father and Myself,* a memoir, Bodley Head, 1968.

Aldrich, Robert. *The Seduction of the Mediterranean: Writing, Art and Homosexual Fantasy,* Routledge, 1993.

Annan, Noel. *Our Age: Portrait of a Generation,* Weidenfeld & Nicolson, 1990.

Bax, Ernest Belfort. *The Ethics of Socialism,* Swan Sonnenschein, 1889.

Beith, Gilbert (editor). *Edward Carpenter: In Appreciation,* George Allen & Unwin, 1931.

Blackwell, Elizabeth. *The Human Element in Sex,* J. & A. Churchill, 1884.

Bland, Lucy. *Banishing the Beast: English Feminism and Sexual Morality 1885–1914,* Penguin, 1995.

Bland, Lucy, and Doan, Laura (editors). *Sexology in Culture: Labelling Bodies and Desires,* Cambridge, Polity Press, 1998.

Bloch, Iwan. *The Sexual Life of Our Times, in its Relation to Modern Civilization,*
trans. Paul Eden, Heinemann, 1920.

Brady, Sean. *Masculinity and Male Homosexuality in Britain 1861–1913,* Palgrave Macmillan, 2005.

Brady, Sean. *John Addington Symonds and Homosexuality: A Critical Edition of Sources,* Palgrave Macmillan, 2012.

Breitmann, Hans (pseud. Charles G. Leland). *The Alternate Sex,* Welby, 1903.

Bronski, Michael. *Culture Clash: The Making of Gay Sensibility,* South End Press, 1984.

Brown, Tony (editor). *Edward Carpenter and Late Victorian Radicalism,* Cass, 1990.

Calder-Marshall, Arthur. *Havelock Ellis: a biography,* 1959.

Chaddock, C. G. (trans.). *Psychopathia Sexualis* by Richard Krafft-Ebing, 7th edition, F A Davis, 1892.

Clews, Colin. *Gay in the 80s,* Matador, 2017.

Costello, John. *Love, Sex and War,* Collins, 1985.

Crozier, Ivan. *Sexual Inversion: Havelock Ellis and John Addington Symonds,* Palgrave Macmillan, 2008.

Croft Cooke, Rupert. *Feasting with Panthers: A New Consideration of Some Late Victorian Writers,* W. H. Allen, 1967.

d'Arch Smith, Timothy. *Love in Earnest,* Routledge & Kegan Paul, 1970.

Davenport-Hines, Richard. *Sex, Death and Punishment,* Collins, 1990.

Ellis, Edith. *The New Horizon in Love and Life,* A. & C. Black, 1921.

Ellis, Edith. *Three Modern Seers,* Stanley Paul & Co., 1910.

Ellis, Havelock. *The New Spirit,* George Bell and Sons, 1890.

Faulks, Sebastian. *The Fatal Englishmen: Three Short Lives,* Vintage, 1996.

Furbank, P. N. *E. M. Forster: A Life,* vol. 2, Secker and Warburg, 1978.

George, Henry. *Progress and Poverty,* Kegan Paul & Co., 1882.

Gosse, Edmund. *Father and Son: A Study of Two Temperaments,* Heinemann, 1907.

Grey, Antony. *Quest for Justice, Towards Homosexual Emancipation,* Sinclair-Stevenson, 1992.

Grosskurth, Phyllis. *Havelock Ellis: A Biography,* Allen Lane, 1980.

Grosskurth, Phyllis. *John Addington Symonds: A Biography,* Longman, 1964.

Harris, Frank. *Oscar Wilde: His Life and Confessions,* Covici Friede, 1930.

Hart-Davis, Rupert. *The Letters of Oscar Wilde,* Butler and Tanner, 1962.

Henderson, Philip. *The Letters of William Morris to His Family and Friends,* Longmans Green & Co. 1950.

Henderson, Archibald. *George Bernard Shaw, Man of the Century,* Appleton-Century-Crofts 1956.

Herdt, Gilbert (editor). *Third Sex, Third Gender: Beyond Sexual Dimorphism in Culture and History,* Zone, 1994.

Higgins, Patrick. *Heterosexual Dictatorship,* Fourth Estate, 1996.

Hirschfeld, Magnus. *Die Homosexualität des Mannes und des Weibes,* 1914.

Hirschfeld, Magnus. *Sapho und Socrates,* 1897.

Hitchens, Richard. *The Green Carnation,* Heinemann, 1894.

Horsfall Allan. 'Battling for Wolfenden', in *Radical Records: Thirty Years of Lesbian and Gay History,* (editors). Cant and Hemmings, Routledge, 1988.

Hyndman, Henry. *The Record of an Adventurous Life,* Macmillan & Co., 1911.

Hyndman, Henry. *The Text Book of Democracy: England for All,* E.W. Allen, 1881.

Irons, Ralph (pseud. Olive Schreiner). *The Story of an African Farm*, Chapman & Hall, 1883.

Kennedy, Hubert. *The Life and Times of Karl Heinrich Ulrichs:* pioneer of the modern gay movement, Alyson Press, 1988.

Largo, M., and Furbank, P. N. (editors). *Selected Letters of E. M. Forster*, Secker and Warburg, 1978.

Laurence, Dan (editor). *Bernard Shaw, Collected Letters 1826–1950*, Viking, 1988.

Lombardi-Nash, Michael (trans.). *The Riddle of 'Man-Manly' Love,* by Karl Heinrich Ulrichs, Prometheus Books, 1994.

Mayhew, Henry. *London Labour and the London Poor*, Woodfall, 1862.

Mayne, Xavier (pseud. Edward Prime-Stevenson). *The Intersexes: A History of Similsexualism as a Problem in Social Life*, privately printed, 1908.

McKenna, Neil. *The Secret Life of Oscar Wilde*, Arrow, 2004.

Mill, John Stuart. *On Liberty*, John W. Parker, 1859.

Miller, Haviland (editor). *The Correspondence of Walt Whitman*, NYUP, 1961–77.

Norton, Rictor. *Mother Clap's Molly House*, Gay Men's Press, 1992.

O'Brien, M. D. *Socialism and Infamy: The Homogenic or Comrade Love Exposed*, privately printed, 1908.

Orwell, George. *The Road to Wigan Pier*, Left Book Club, 1937.

Orwell, Sonia, and Secker, Angus (editors). *George Orwell, Collected Journalism and Letters*, Secker and Warburg, 1968.

Proctor, Dennis (editor), *The Autobiography of Goldsworthy Lowes Dickinson and other unpublished writings*, Duckworth, 1973.

Robinson, Paul. *The Modernization of Sex: Havelock Ellis, Alfred Kinsey, William Masters and Virginia Johnson*, Elek, 1976.

Rossetti, W. M. (editor), *Walt Whitman: Selected Poems*, Chatto & Windus, 1868.

Rowbotham, Sheila, and Weeks, Jeffrey. *Socialism and the New Life: The Personal and Sexual Politics of Edward Carpenter and Havelock Ellis*, Pluto Press, 1977.

Rowbotham, Sheila. *Edward Carpenter, A Life of Liberty and Love*, Verso, 2008.

Salt, H. S., *Company I Have Kept*, Allen & Unwin, 1930.

Salt, H. S., *Seventy Years Among Savages*, Allen & Unwin, 1921.

Shively, Charley. *Calamus Lovers: Walt Whitman's Working-class Camerados*, Gay Sunshine Press, 1987.

Showalter, Elaine. *Sexual Anarchy: Gender and Culture at the Fin de Siécle*, Viking, 1990.

Simpson, Colin. *The Cleveland Street Affair*, Weidenfeld & Nicolson, 1977.

Smith, Helen. *Masculinity, Class and Same-Sex Desire in Industrial England, 1895–1957*, Palgrave Macmillan, 2015.

Thiele, Beverly. 'Coming of Age, Edward Carpenter on Sex and Reproduction', in *Edward Carpenter and Late Victorian Radicalism*, ed. T. Brown, Frank Cass, 1990.

Traubel, Horace Logo. *With Walt Whitman in Camden*, Gay and Bird, 1906.

Tsuzuki, Chushichi. *Edward Carpenter: Prophet of Human Fellowship*, CUP, 1980.

Weeks, Jeffrey. *Coming Out: Homosexual Politics in Britain from the Nineteenth Century to the Present*, Quartet Books, 1990.

Weeks, Jeffrey, and Porter, Kevin (editors). *Between the Acts: Lives of Homosexual Men, 1885–1967*, Rivers Oram Press, London, 1998.

Weininger, Otto. *Sex and Character*, Heinemann, 1910.

Westwood, Gordon. *Society and the Homosexual*, Victor Gollancz, 1952.

Whitman, Walt. *Song of the Open Road*, Limited Edition Club, 1990.

Wilde, Oscar. *Phrases and Philosophies for the Use of the Young*, Gay and Bird, 1894.

Wildeblood, Peter. *A Way of Life,* Weidenfeld & Nicolson, 1956.

Wildeblood, Peter. *Against the Law*, Harmondsworth, 1957.

Winsten, Stephen. *Salt and His Circle*, Hutchinson, 1951.

Notes

CHAPTER 1

1   *My Days and Dreams*, Charles Scribner & Sons, 1916, pp. 320–321.
2   'Desirable Mansions', in *England's Ideal*, 1887, p. 86.
3   *Towards Democracy*, George Allen & Unwin, 1905, p. 124.
4   *My Days and Dreams*, Charles Scribner & Son, 1916, p. 38.
5   *My Days and Dreams*, pp. 40–41.
6   Ibid., p. 13.
7   Ibid., p. 14.
8   Ida Hyett, in Gilbert Beith, ed., *Edward Carpenter: In Appreciation*, George Allen & Unwin, 1931, p. 114.
9   Witness, Edmund Gosse, in his memoir *Father and Son*, and Samuel Butler in his semi-autobiographical novel, *The Way of All Flesh*.
10 In a reply to a congratulatory address on his seventieth birthday. CC.
11 *My Days and Dreams*, p. 28.
12 Ibid., pp. 13–14.
13 Phyllis Grosskurth, ed., *The Memoirs of John Addington Symonds*, Random House, 1984, p. 82.
14 *My Days and Dreams*, p. 29.
15 Phyllis Grosskurth, *The Memoirs of John Addington Symonds*, p. 94.
16 Case V1 in Havelock Ellis's *Sexual Inversion*, 1897.
17 *My Days and Dreams*, p. 30.
18 Ibid., p. 25.
19 Edward Carpenter to Charles Carpenter, 13 July 1864, CC. 339/4.
20 Ibid., 23 July 1864, CC. 339/5.
21 Charles Carpenter to his father, CC. 349/67.

CHAPTER 2

1   *My Days and Dreams*, p. 63.
2   Ibid., p. 77.
3   *My Days and Dreams*, early draft, CC. mss. 198, p. 71.
4   *My Days and Dreams*, p. 63.
5   Ibid., p. 63.
6   Unpublished manuscript, CC. 44.
7   *The Intermediate Sex*: A Study of Some Transitional Types of Men and Women, Swan Sonnenschein, 1908. p. 62.
8   Unpublished manuscript, CC. mss.1.
9   *My Days and Dreams*, p. 205.
10 Leslie Stephen, *Some Early Impressions*, L & V Woolf, 1924, p. 67.
11 Edward Carpenter to Charles Carpenter, March 28 1867, CC. 339/7.
12 Charles Carpenter to Edward Carpenter, June 30 1867, CC. 349/68.
13 Edward Carpenter to Charles Carpenter, 28 March 1867, CC. 339/7.
14 *The Religious Influence of Art*, Deighton Bell & Co., Cambridge, 1870.
15 *Poems By Walt Whitman*, selected and edited by William Michael Rossetti, John Camden Hotten, 1868.
16 Ibid.
17 *My Days and Dreams*, p. 65.
18 Ibid., p. 30.
19 Rossetti, Op. cit.
20 Ibid., p. 86.
21 Reply to congratulatory address on his seventieth birthday.
22 *My Days and Dreams*, p. 65.
23 Rossetti, Op. cit.
24 Walt Whitman, *Democratic Vistas*, Liberal Arts, 1949, p. 328.
25 *England's Ideal*, p. 2.
26 *My Days and Dreams*, p. 65.
27 'Art and Democracy', in *Angel's Wings*, Swan Sonnenschein, 1898, p. 10.
28 *My Days and Dreams*, p. 52.
29 Ibid., p. 58.
30 Unpublished sermons, CC. 2/9.
31 Carpenter to J N Dalton, 29 October 1871, John Dalton Papers, Worcester College Oxford.
32 Elizabeth Carpenter to Edward Carpenter, 3 February 1871, CC. 342/26.
33 Unpublished sermons, CC. 2/1.
34 Unpublished manuscript. CC. mss. 1.
35 Ben Pimlott, *Hugh Dalton*, Harper Collins, 1985, pp. 78–9.
36 *My Days and Dreams*, p. 251.
37 In *My Days and Dreams* Beck is disguised as 'Edward Brown' as he was still alive when it was published in 1916.

38	Havelock Ellis, *Sexual Inversion*, case V1.
39	*My Days and Dreams*, early draft, CC. 200.
40	Beck to Carpenter, 27 March 1871, CC. 386/7.
41	Carpenter to Charles Oates, 5 September 1871, CC. 351/3.
42	Carpenter to Oates, 19 December 1870, CC. 351/2.
43	Carpenter to Oates, 4 February 1871, CC. 351/5.
44	Carpenter to Oates, 5 September 1871, CC. 351/3.
45	Beck to Carpenter, 1 September 1871, CC. 386/8.
46	Ibid.
47	Carpenter to Oates, 10 November 1871, CC. 351/3.
48	Carpenter to Oates, 15 November 1871, CC. 351/4.
49	Ibid.
50	Ibid.
51	Oates to Carpenter, 1 February 1872, CC. 352/1.
52	Oates to Carpenter, 7 April 1872, CC. 352/2.
53	Carpenter to Oates, 27 April 1872, CC. 351/6.
54	Robert Aldrich, *The Seduction of the Mediterranean*: Writing, Art and Homosexual Fantasy. Routledge, 1993, p. 101.
55	Henry Salt, *Seventy Years Among Savages*, Allan & Unwin, 1921, p. 130.
56	*My Days and Dreams*, p. 72.
57	Ibid., pp. 69–70.
58	Jane Daubeney to Carpenter, November 1872, CC. mss. 198.
59	Carpenter to Oates, 30 December 1872, CC. 351/7.
60	*My Days and Dreams*, p. 67.
61	Ibid., p. 68.
62	Carpenter to Oates, 13 June 1873, CC. 351/2.
63	CC. mss. 2/2.
64	*The Drama of Love and Death*, G Allen & Co., 1912, p. 29.
65	*Towards Democracy*, p. 35.
66	*My Days and Dreams*, p. 70.
67	Ibid.
68	*Narcissus and Other Poems*, Henry S King and Co, 1873.
69	Carpenter to Oates, 30 October 1873, CC. 351/14.
70	Walt Whitman, *Song of the Open Road*, Limited Editions Club, New York, 1990.
71	*My Days and Dreams*, p. 77.
72	Whitman, *Leaves of Grass*, Michael Moon (editor), W.W. Norton, 2002, p. 39.
73	Edward Carpenter, *Days with Walt Whitman*, George Allen, 1906, p. 58.
74	Carpenter to Oates, 20 July 1874, CC. 351/17.
75	Horace Traubel, *With Walt Whitman in Camden*, Boston, 1906, pp. 159–161.

76   Ibid.

77   Ibid.

78   *My Days and Dreams*, p. 30.

79   Traubel, op. cit.

80   Horace Traubel, *With Walt Whitman in Camden*, March 28–July 14, 1888, pp. 159–61.

CHAPTER 3

1   *Towards Democracy*, pp. 6–7.

2   *My Days and Dreams*, pp. 85–6.

3   Ibid., p. 88.

4   *Days with Walt Whitman*, George Allen, 1906, p. 30.

5   Ibid., p. 6.

6   Ibid., p. 5.

7   Neil McKenna, *The Secret Life of Oscar Wilde*, Arrow, 2005, p. 28.

8   Charley Shively, *Calamus Lovers: Walt Whitman's Working-class Camerados*, 1987.

9   *My Days and Dreams*, p. 9.

10   *My Days and Dreams*, p. 104.

11   Ibid., p.103.

12   Ibid., p.104.

13   Ibid.

14   Ibid., p. 251.

15   Ibid., p. 209.

16   Ibid., p. 106.

17   Carpenter to Whitman, 16 March 1882, Traubel, p. 252.

18   *My Days and Dreams*, p. 201.

19   Timothy d'Arch Smith, *Love in Earnest*, Routledge Kegan Paul, 1970, p. 18.

20   Garry Schmidgall, *Walt Whitman, A Gay Life*, 1997, p. xx.

21   Carpenter to Oates, 27 November 1882, CC. 351/34.

22   Carpenter to Whitman, 2 March 1884, Traubel, D Appleton & Co., 1908, pp. 76–77.

23   'In the Drawing Rooms', *Towards Democracy*, p. 139.

24   Henry Salt, *Company I Have Kept*, p. 54.

25   *My Days and Dreams*, p. 164.

26   Walter Seward, *A Very Small Tribute to a Very Great Friend*, in Beith, p. 203.

CHAPTER 4

1   *Homogenic Love*, p. 155. (Uranian is a term for homosexual.)

2   *Sexual Inversion*, case V1.
3   James Blyth, *Edward Fitzgerald and Posh*, John Long, 1908, p. 7.
4   Dennis Proctor, ed., *The Autobiography of G Lowes Dickinson*, Duckworth, 1973, p. 72.
5   Noel Annan, *Our Age: Portrait of a Generation*, Weidenfeld & Nicolson, p.109.
6   J. R. Ackerley (Joe Randolph), *My Father and Myself*, Bodley Head, 1986, p. 131.
7   Phyllis Grosskurth, ed., *The Memoirs of John Addington Symonds*, Random House, 1984, p. 254.
8   Ibid., p. 254.
9   Ibid., p. 267.
10   Symonds to Charles Kains-Jackson, 30 October 1892, *Letters* (editors) Schueller & Peters, Wayne State University Press, vol. 111.
11   Symonds to Carpenter, 21 January 1893, *Letters* vol. 111, p. 808.

CHAPTER 5

1   *My Days and Dreams*, early draft, CC. mss. 200.
2   Ibid.
3   *Towards Democracy*, XLV.
4   Ibid., p. 217.
5   Hukin to Carpenter, 8 July 1886, CC. 262/5.
6   Hukin to Carpenter, 28 Oct 1886, CC. 262/6.
7   Carpenter to Oates, 20 December 1886, CC. 351/3.
8   Helen Smith, *Masculinity, Class and Same-Sex Desire in Industrial England 1895–1957*, Palgrave Macmillan, 2015, p. 70.
9   Hukin to Carpenter, 17 January 1887, CC. 362/7.
10   Carpenter to Oates, 10 April 1887, CC. 351/38.
11   Carpenter to Hukin, 15 May 1887, CC. 362/9.
12   Hukin to Carpenter, 15 May 1867, CC. 362/9.
13   Hukin to Carpenter, 24 May 1887, CC. 362/11.
14   Carpenter to Hukin, Whit Monday 1887, CC. 361/3.
15   Carpenter to Hukin, 1 June 1887, CC. 361/4.
16   Ibid.
17   Hukin to Carpenter, 1 June 1887, CC. 362/13.
18   Carpenter to Hukin, 3 June 1887, CC. 351/5.
19   Carpenter to Charles Oates, 3 June 1887, CC. 351/40.
20   Hukin to Carpenter, 21 November 1887, CC. 362/16.
21   Sheila Rowbotham, in Sheila Rowbotham and Jeffrey Weeks, *Socialism and the New Life: The Personal and Sexual Politics of Edward Carpenter and Havelock Ellis*, Pluto Press, 1977, p. 81.

22 Ibid., p. 122.
23 *Towards Democracy*, p. 413.
24 Carpenter to Charles Oates, 27 August 1887, CC. 351/42.
25 Carpenter to Charles Oates, 19 December 1887, CC. 351/43.
26 Charles Ashbee, Journal, The London Library, 11–12 December 1885.
27 Ibid., 26 July 1886.
28 McKenna, op. cit. p. 291.
29 *The Intermediate Sex*, p. 14.

CHAPTER 6

1 Scotland had to wait until 1980 and Northern Ireland until 1982 for similar legislation.

CHAPTER 7

1 *My Days and Dreams*, pp. 245, 247, 128.
2 Manuscript Notes for Lecture, CC. mss. 27.
3 *My Days and Dreams*, p. 20.
4 *Desirable Mansions*, 'Progress', June 1883.
5 *My Days and Dreams*, p. 83.
6 *Edward Carpenter's Message to His Age*, The Forum, August 1911.
7 John Haywood, Manchester, 1883.
8 'Today', *England's Ideal*, May 1884.
9 *Justice*, February 1885.
10 'Today', February 1885.
11 *Edward Carpenter's Message to His Age*, The Forum, August 1911.
12 *England's Ideal and other papers on social subjects*, Swan Sonnenschein, 1887.
13 *The Pioneer*, January 1889.
14 *Civilisation: Its Cause and Cure, and other essays*, Swan Sonnenschein & Co, 1889.
15 'Social Progress and Individual Effort', in *England's Ideal*, Swan Sonnenschein, 1887, p. 67.
16 Henry George, *Progress and Poverty*, Kegan Paul & Co, 1882.
17 Archibald Henderson, *George Bernard Shaw*, Hurst & Blackett, 1911, p. 9.
18 Henry Hyndman, *The Text-Book of Democracy: England for All*, E.W. Allen, 1881.
19 *My Days and Dreams*, p. 114.
20 Henry Hyndman, *The Record of an Adventurous Life*, Macmillan & Co., 1911, p. 334.
21 Quoted in Winsten, *Salt and His Circle*, p. 64.
22 *My Days and Dreams*, p. 246.

23 *Civilisation: Its Cause and Cure*, pp. 107–8.

24 P. Henderson, ed., *The Letters of William Morris to His Family and Friends*, 1950, p. 223.

25 *The Clarion*, November 1884.

26 *My Days and Dreams*, p. 21.

27 Havelock Ellis, *My Life*, William Heinemann Limited, 1930, p. 163.

28 Ibid.

29 R. Blatchford to Carpenter, 11 January 1894, CC. 386/46.

30 *The Clarion*, 19 December 1902.

31 J. Bruce Glasier, Diary, 25 January 1903, quoted in Tsuzuki Chushichi, Edward Carpenter: Prophet of Human Fellowship,1980, p. 143.

32 G. B. Shaw, *Collected Letters*, ed. Dan H. Laurence, vol. 2, 1972, p. 890.

33 E. Belfort Bax, *The Ethics of Socialism*, Swan Sonnenschein, 1893, p. 62.

34 'Sexual Ethical Twaddle', the *Social Democrat*, June 1899, pp. 165–8.

35 George Orwell, *Collected Essays, Journalism and Letters*, ed. Sonia Orwell and Ian Angus, Secker and Warburg, 1968, p. 72.

36 George Orwell, *The Road to Wigan Pier*, Left Book Club, 1937, p. 206.

CHAPTER 8

1 Olive Schreiner to Havelock Ellis, 2 May 1884, Cronwright-Schreiner Letters, p. 17.

2 Edward Carpenter to Havelock Ellis, 24 October 1885, HRC.

3 *My Days and Dreams*, p. 227.

4 Schreiner to Carpenter, 1 April 1887, CC. 359/4.

5 Richard Rive, ed., *The Letters of Olive Schreiner*, vol. 1, p. 122.

6 Schreiner to Carpenter, 1 April 1887, CC. 359/4.

7 Schreiner to Carpenter, 16 April 1888, CC. 358/21.

8 Schreiner to Carpenter, 3 January 1887, Rive, Letters, p. 118.

9 Karl Pearson, *The Ethics of Freethought*, T. Fisher Unwin, 1888, p. 393.

10 'To-Day', February 1887, and in *The Ethics of Freethought*, T. Fisher Unwin, 1888, p. 445.

11 Ibid., p. 440.

CHAPTER 9

1 Edward Carpenter, *The Drama of Love and Death*: A Study in Human Evolution, George Allen & Unwin, 1912, p. 63.

2 *My Days and Dreams*, p. 195.

3 *My Days and Dreams*, p. 197.

4 *Love's Coming of Age*, Methuen & Co. 1896, p. 36.

5 Ibid., pp. 2–3.

6   Lucy Bland, *Banishing the Beast: English Feminism and Sexual Morality 1885–1914*.

7   Havelock Ellis, *Man and Woman*: A Study of Human Secondary Sexual Characteristics, A & C Black, 1894.

8   Gagnier, *Idylls of the Market Place*, p. 160, quoted in Elaine Showalter, Sexual Anarchy: Gender and Culture at the *Fin de Siécle*, Viking, 1990 p. 174.

9   *Love's Coming of Age*, p. 63.

10   Beverly Thiele, *'Coming of Age: Edward Carpenter on Sex and Reproduction'*, in Tony Brown (editor), *Edward Carpenter and Late Victorian Radicalism*, Cass 1990, pp. 107–8.

11   Ibid., pp. 107–8.

12   Ibid., p. 101.

13   *Love's Coming of Age*, p. 45.

14   Ibid., pp. 46–7.

15   *Towards Democracy*, p. 92.

16   *Love's Coming of Age*, p. 56.

17   Kate Salt to Carpenter, 17 February 1897, CC. 355/15.

18   Elaine Showalter, *Sexual Anarchy Gender and Culture at the Fin de Siécle*, Viking, 1990, p. 175.

19   *The Intermediate Sex*, p. 35.

20   Schreiner to Carpenter, 6 April 1888, CC. 259/18.

21   Schreiner to Carpenter, 21 March 1889, CC. 359/39.

CHAPTER 10

1   *Forschungen über das Rätsel der mann-männlichen Liebe. The Riddle of 'Man-Manly' Love*, translated by Michael A Lombardi-Nash, Prometheus Books, 1994.

2   See Hubert Kennedy, *'Karl Heinrich Ulrichs First Theorist of Homosexuality'*, in *Science and Homosexualities*, edited by Vernon Rosario, Routledge, 1996.

3   Lombardi-Nash, vol. 2, p. 636.

4   Lombardi-Nash, vol. 1, p. 40.

5   Ibid.

6   Lombardi-Nash, vol. 2, pp. 604–5.

7   Kennedy, op. cit., p. 39.

8   See Rictor Norton's *Mother Clap's Molly House*, Gay Men's Press, 1992.

CHAPTER 11

1   Havelock Ellis, *The New Spirit*, George Bell & Sons, 1890.

2   Symonds to Ellis, 6 May 1890, Letters, vol. 111, p. 458.

3   Havelock Ellis, *The New Spirit*, pages 122 and 127.
4   Symonds to Horace Traubel, 27 February 1892, Letters, vol. 111, p. 667.
5   Symonds to Graham Dakyns, 22 August 1868, Letters, vol. 1, p. 837.
6   Symonds to Carpenter, 29 September 1892, Letters, vol. 111, p.797.
7   Ellis to Carpenter, 17 December 1892, CC. 357/5.
8   I give a full account of their collaboration in my book, *The Fraternity of the Estranged, The Fight for Homosexual Rights in England, 1891–1908*, Matador, 2018.

CHAPTER 12

1   Colin Simpson, *The Cleveland Street Affair*, Weidenfeld & Nicolson, 1977, p. 3.
2   Timothy d'Arch Smith, *Love in Earnest*, p. xxii.
3   *Teleny or the Reverse of the Medal, A physiological romance of today*. Cosmopoli, 1893.
4   *The Yellow Book*: an illustrated quarterly, 1894–97, Elkin Mathews and John Lane.
5   Richard Davenport-Hines, *Sex, Death and Punishment: attitudes to sex and sexuality in Britain since the Renaissance*, Collins, 1990, p. 126.
6   *The Green Carnation*: edited with an introduction by Stanley Weintraub, University of Nebraska Press, 1970, p. xiii.
7   *Pall Mall Gazette*, 2 October 1894.
8   *The Chameleon*, edited by John Francis Bloxam, Gray and Bird, 1894.
9   *Contemporary Review*, Number 67, 1895.

CHAPTER 13

1   *Homogenic Love and its Place in a Free Society* p. 16…
2   Noel Annan, *Our Age: Portrait of a Generation*, p. 107.
3   *My Days and Dreams*, p. 195.
4   Ibid., p. 195.
5   *Homogenic Love*, p. 12.
6   *Homogenic Love*, p. 32.
7   Ibid., p. 31.
8   Ibid., p. 27.
9   Ibid., p. 18.
10   Ibid., p. 18.
11   Ibid., p. 18.
12   Ibid., p. 15.
13   Ibid., p. 15.
14   Ibid., p. 16.

15   Ibid., p. 34

16   Ibid., pp. 42/44.

17   Ibid., p. 44.

18   Ibid., p. 48.

19   Ibid., p. 51.

20   Ibid., p. 50.

21   Brown to Carpenter, 14 February 1895, CC. 386/52.

22   Ibid.

23   *The Autobiography of Goldsworthy Lowes Dickinson and other unpublished writings*, Duckworth, 1973, p. 104.

24   Ibid., p. 157.

25   *Humanity*, vol. 1, April 1895.

CHAPTER 14

1   *My Days and Dreams*, p. 197.

2   Frank Harris, *Oscar Wilde: His Life and Confessions*, Covici Friede, 1930, p. 171.

3   *Evening News*, 5 April 1895.

4   *Westminster Gazette*, 6 April 1895.

5   *Daily Telegraph*, 6 April 1895.

6   *National Observer*, 6 April 1895.

7   *Review of Reviews*, 15 June 1895.

8   Edward Carpenter, 'Some Recent Criminal Cases', *Freedom*, June 1895.

9   *Labour Leader*, 13 June 1895.

10   *Justice*, 13 April 1895.

11   Carpenter to Ellis, 28 June 1895, HRC.

12   'Edward Carpenter's Tracts on Sex', *The Humanitarian*, 2 August 1895.

13   Rupert Hart-Davis, *The Letters of Oscar Wilde*, Butler and Tanner, 1962, p. 414.

14   Neil McKenna, *The Secret Life of Oscar Wilde*, Arrow, 2004, p. 376.

15   *My Days and Dreams*, p. 196.

16   Carpenter to George Hukin, 31 July 1895, CC. 361/25.

17   Carpenter to Ellis, 14 October 1895, HRC.

18   Carpenter to Ellis, 15 January 1896, HRC.

19   Carpenter to Oates, 14 March 1896, CC. 351/66.

20   *Love's Coming of Age*, Manchester Labour Press, 1896.

21   Lily Bell, *The Labour Leader*, 27 June 1896.

22   Schreiner to Carpenter, 8 October 1894, CC. 359/73.

23   Ellis to Carpenter, 22 January 1894, CC. 357/6.

24   Ellis to Carpenter, 24 April 1896, CC. 357/7.

25   Edith Ellis to Carpenter, 20 April 1896, CC. 358/3.

26   Edith Ellis, *The New Horizon in Love and Life*, Blackblocks, 1921.
27   Carpenter to Ellis, 28 April 1896, HRC.
28   Carpenter to Ellis, 20 July 1896, HRC.
29   Edward Carpenter, *An Unknown People*, A & H Bonner, 1897.
30   'An Unknown People', *The Reformer*, July 1897, p, 14.
31   Ibid., pp. 14–15.
32   Ibid., p. 17.
33   Ibid., p. 16.

CHAPTER 15

1   Carpenter to Ellis, 19 April 1895, HRC.
2   Carpenter to Ellis, 28 June 1895, HRC.
3   Havelock Ellis, *My Life*, p. 297.
4   Ibid., p. 296.
5   Carpenter to Ellis, 2 December 1896, HRC.
6   Havelock Ellis, *My Life*, p. 297.
7   Havelock Ellis and John Addington Symonds, *Studies in the Psychology of Sex*, vol. 1, *Sexual Inversion*, Wilson and Macmillan, 1897.
8   Brown to Ellis, 8 August 1895, HRC.
9   Carpenter to Kate Salt, 31 August 1897, CC. 354/49.
10   Horatio Brown to Carpenter, 21 November 1897, CC. 386/76.
11   Ibid.
12   Ivan Crozier, *Sexual Inversion, A Critical Edition*, Palgrave Macmillan, 2008, p. 93.
13   Ibid.
14   Ellis to Carpenter, 3 August 1897, CC. 357/8.
15   Havelock Ellis, *Studies in the Psychology of Sex*, vol. 1, *Sexual Inversion*, The University Press limited, 1897.
16   Carpenter to Ellis, 27 November 1897, HRC.
17   *The Adult*, vol. 1, May 1897.
18   Dan H. Laurence, *Bernard Shaw: Collected Letters*, ed. Max Reinhardt, 1972, pp. 57–8.
19   Havelock Ellis, *A Note on the Bedborough Trial* (privately printed).
20   *The Lancet*, 19 November 1897.
21   Recounted by Phyllis Grosskurth, in *Havelock Ellis: A Biography*, Allen Lane, 1980, p. 187.
22   Huston Peterson, *Havelock Ellis: Philosopher of Love* (verbatim report of the trial), Houghton Mifflin, 1928.
23   Ellis, *My Life*, p. 315.
24   *A Note on the Bedborough Trial*.
25   Ibid.

26   *Sexual Inversion*, p. 147.

27   *Sexual Inversion*, case V111, p. 61.

28   Ibid., p. 62.

29   Ibid., pp. 156–157.

30   Ibid., pp. 156–157.

31   Ibid., p. 154.

32   Ibid., pp. 145–146.

33   Symonds, *A Problem in Modern Ethics*, 1892, p. 4.

34   Francis Galton, *Hereditary Genius, an inquiry into its laws and consequences*, London, 1869. Galton was a cousin of Charles Darwin.

35   Havelock Ellis, *The Task of Social Hygiene*, Constable, 1912, p. 200.

36   Havelock Ellis, 'The Individual and the Race', in *Essays on Love and Virtue in Morals, Manners and Men*, Watts & Co, 1939, pp. 6–7.

37   Ibid.

38   *Sexual Inversion*, p. 155.

39   Magnus Hirschfeld, *The Homosexuality of Man and Woman* (Die Homosexualität des Mannes und des Weibes), 1914.

40   Iwan Bloch, *The Sex Life of our Times in its Relation to Modern Civilization* (Das Sexualleben unserer Zeit in seinen Beziehungen zur modermen Kultur), 1907.

41   Sexual Inversion,146.

42   Ibid., p. 144.

43   Phyllis Grosskurth, *Havelock Ellis*: A Biography, 1980, p. 187.

44   Paul Robinson, *The Modernisation of Sex*, Elek, 1976, p. 4.

45   Ivan Crozier, *Sexual Inversion, Havelock Ellis and John Addington Symonds*, p. 29.

46   Ellis, *Sexual Inversion*, p. 158.

CHAPTER 16

1   Unpublished manuscripts, CC. number 44.

2   Carpenter to Oates, 23 February 1890.

3   *My Days and Dreams*, p. 209.

4   Carpenter to Oates, 23 February 1890, CC. 351/53.

5   Arunachalam to Carpenter, 25 November 1888, CC. 372/37.

6   Arunachalam to Carpenter, 27 December 1889, CC. 372/39.

7   *Light from The East*, p. 15.

8   Hukin to Carpenter, 10 October 1890, CC. 362/37.

9   To be published as From *Adam's Peak to Elephanta*, Swan Sonnenschein & Co. Limited, 1892.

10   *Ibid.,* p. 27.

11   Carpenter to Oates, 7 December 1890, CC. 351/6.

12   Carpenter to Kate Salt, 5 November 1890, CC. 354/10.
13   *From Adam's Peak to Elephanta*, p. 148.
14   *My Days and Dreams*, p. 143.
15   Ibid., p. 144.
16   *From Adam's Peak to Elephanta*, p. 324.
17   *My Days and Dreams*, p. 145.
18   Parminder Kaur Bakshi, 'Homosexuality and Orientalism, Edward Carpenter's Journey to the East', in Brown, (editor), *Edward Carpenter and Late Victorian Radicalism*.
19   *From Adam's Peak to Elephanta*, p. 123.
20   Ibid., p. 163, p.175.
21   Ibid., p. 163.

CHAPTER 17

1   In *The Intersexes*, Xavier Mayne described it as 'the Gaze'; a kind of psycho-sexual interrogation.
2   Carpenter, George Merrill, A True History and Study in Psychology, 1913, CC. 363/17.
3   *My Days and Dreams*, p. 159.
4   Ellis, *Sexual Inversion*, pp. 46–47.
5   Jeffrey Weeks, *Coming Out*, Quartet Books, 1990, p. 79.
6   Ellis, *Sexual Inversion*, pp. 46–47.
7   George Merrill, A True History
8   Ellis, *Sexual Inversion*, p. 46–47.
9   *The Intermediate Sex*, p. 186.
10   Timothy d'Arch Smith, *Love in Ernest*, p. 18.
11   Carpenter to Oates, 14 July 1897, CC. 351/75.
12   *Towards Democracy*, p. 416.
13   George Merrill, A True History.
14   *Irish Citizen*, 12 June 1915.
15   Carpenter to Hukin, 9 January 1895, CC. 361/17.
16   Merrill to Carpenter, 26 October 1896, CC. 363/3.
17   *The Drama of Love and Death*, p. 63.
18   Notes on George Merrill.
19   *The Drama of Love and Death*, p. 66.
20   Noel Annan, *Our Age*, p. 11.
21   Carpenter to Kate Salt, 10 December 1897, CC. 354/52.
22   *My Days and Dreams*, p. 34.
23   Harold Picton, in Beith, p. 169.
24   Quoted by Steven Winsten in *Salt and His Circle*, pp. 186–7.
25   *My Days and Dreams*, p. 161.

26   Ibid., p. 164.
27   George Merrill, A True History.
28   Ibid.
29   'Personal Impressions of Edward Carpenter', in *Three Modern Seers*, Stanley Paul & Company, 1910, pp. 11–12.
30   George Merrill, A True History.

CHAPTER 18

1   Edward Carpenter, *The Intermediate Sex, A Study of Some Transitional Types of Men and Women*, Allen & Unwin, 1908.
2   *The Intermediate Sex*, p. 79.
3   Magnus Hirschfeld, *Sapho and Socrates* (Sapho und Socrates), 1896.
4   Otto Weininger, *Geschlect und Charakter*, 1903.
5   Hans Breitmann, pseud. Charles G. Leland, *The Alternate Sex*, Welby,1903.
6   Xavier Mayne, pseud. Edward Prime-Stevenson, *The Intersexes*, privately printed, 1908.
7   Symonds, *Memoirs*, p. 64.
8   Ellis, Sexual *Inversion*, p. 132.
9   *The Intermediate Sex*, pp. 18–19.
10   Ibid., p. 19.
11   Ibid., p. 32.
12   *The Intermediate Sex*, p. 57.
13   Ibid., p. 2.
14   Gert Hekma, in Gilbert Herdt, editor, *Third Sex, Third Gender: Beyond Sexual Dimorphism in Culture and History*, p. 236.
15   *The Intermediate Sex*, p. 40.
16   Ibid., p. 70.
17   Ibid., pp. 22–23
18   *Some Friends of Walt Whitman*, p. 16.

CHAPTER 19

1   M. D. O'Brien, *Socialism and Infamy: The Homogenic or Comrade Love Exposed: An Open Letter in Plain Words for a Socialist Prophet*, privately printed, 1909.
2   Hukin to Carpenter, 11 April 1909, CC. 362/100.
3   Hukin to Carpenter, 11 April 1909, CC. 362/101.
4   Carpenter to Hukin, 23 June 1909, CC. 361/50.
5   Henry Salt, *Company I Have Kept*, Allen & Unwin, p. 60.

CHAPTER 20

1   Edward Carpenter, *Intermediate Types among Primitive Folk*, 1914.

2   *The Drama of Love and Death* (1912) and *Pagan and Christian Creeds* (1920).

3   Jeffrey Weeks, *Coming Out: Homosexual Politics in Britain from the Nineteenth Century to the Present*, Quartet Books, 1977, p. 128.

4   Stella Browne (1880–1955), feminist, sex radical and birth control campaigner.

5   Weeks, *Coming Out*, p. 136.

6   Allan Horsfall, 'Battling for Wolfenden', in *Radical Records: Thirty Years of Lesbian and Gay History*, (editors). Cant and Hemmings, Routledge, 1988, p. 18.

7   Patrick Higgins, *Heterosexual Dictatorship*, Fourth Estate, 1996, p. 181. Higgins describes over fifty trials held up and down the country, of both the high and the lowly.

8   See Helen Smith, *Masculinity, Class and Same-Sex Desire in Industrial England, 1895–1957*, Palgrave Macmillan, 2015. Smith shows that same-sex desire could be part of everyday life in working-class communities.

9   Jeffrey Weeks, *Coming Out*, p. 163.

10   Gordon Westwood, *Society and the Homosexual*, Victor Gollancz, 1952, p. 68.

11   Peter Wildeblood, *Against the Law*, Harmondsworth, 1955.

12   Peter Wildeblood, *A Way of Life*, Weidenfeld and Nicolson, 1956.

13   Sebastian Faulks, *The Fatal Englishmen: Three Short Lives*, Vintage, 1996.

14   Patrick Higgins, *Heterosexual Dictatorship*, 89.

15   Antony Grey, *Quest For Justice: Towards Homosexual Emancipation*, Sinclair-Stevenson, 1992pp. 1–2.

16   Jeffrey Weeks, *Coming Out*, p. 156.

17   Gray, *Quest for Justice*, pp. 1–2.

18   Quoted by Patrick Higgins, in *Heterosexual Dictatorship*, p. 2.

19   Colin Clews, *Gay in the 80s*, Matador, 2017, p. 102.

20   Reported in *The Times*, 28 July 1967.

21   Jeffrey Weeks, *Coming Out*, p. 156.

22   *The Intermediate Sex*, p. 15.

23   *The Intermediate Sex*, p. 82.

CHAPTER 21

1   MacDonald to Carpenter, 26 July 1924, CC. 386/404.

2   Seward to Carpenter, 30 June 1910, CC. 370/1.

3   Bishop to Carpenter, 10 August 1903, CC. 365/8.

4   *Between the Acts: Lives of Homosexual Men, 1885–1967*, edited by Jeffrey

Weeks and Kevin Porter, Rivers Oram Press, 1991.

5   Carpenter to Clemas, 27 November 1916, CC. 390/6.

6   Steven Winsten, *Salt and His Circle*, p. 161.

7   E. M. Forster, *Commonplace Book*, Philip Gardner (editor), Scolar Press, 1 1978, p. 52.

8   Winsten, p. 162.

9   Gilbert Beith, editor, *Edward Carpenter: In Appreciation*, George Allen & Unwin, 1931, p. 32.

10 Winsten, p. 162.

11 Beith, p. 110.

12 E. M. Forster, The Life and Works of Edward Carpenter, BBC Book Talk, 25 September 1944, CC. 387-5.

13 Forster to Gilbert Beith, 14 March 1944, CC. 387/1.

14 Carpenter to Forster, 23 August 1914, *Selected Letters*, vol. 1, p. 223.

15 P. N. Furbank, *E. M. Forster: A Life*, vol. 2, Secker and Warburg, 1978, p. 25.

16 Quoted in *Salt and His Circle*, p. 1.

Index

The abbreviation EC refers to Edward Carpenter.

Index